★ ★ ★

Hollywood Lovers

★ ★ ★

Hollywood Lovers

EDITED BY
SHERIDAN McCOID

ORION
MEDIA

First published in 1997 by Orion Media
An imprint of Orion Books Ltd
Orion House, 5 Upper St Martin's Lane, London WC2H 9EA

Project Editor: Natasha Martyn-Johns
Designed by The Bridgewater Book Company Ltd

A CIP catalogue record for this book is available
from the British Library.

ISBN 0-75281-035-9

Litho Origination By Pixel Colour Ltd London.
Printed and bound in Italy
By Printer Trento SRL and L.E.G.O., Vicenza

★

CONTENTS

CAST LIST
IN ORDER OF APPEARANCE

GENA LEE NOLIN, *actress*, Baywatch
JOAN RIVERS, *comedienne*
STEPHANIE BEACHAM, *actress*
ARLENE, *comedienne*
CHRISTINE O'KEEFE, *Beverly Hills matchmaker*
ROGER CLINTON, *brother of Bill*
DR RACHEL COPELAN,
couples counsellor and hypnotherapist
DIANE CONWAY, *comedienne and*
self-appointed Fairy Godmother of
dating and mating
JACKIE COLLINS, *author*
RITA RUDNER, *comedienne*
DENISE GILBERT, *Miss Flirt USA,*
a title awarded by American Singles
RICHARD GOSS, *Chairman of American Singles*
PHYLLIS DILLER, *comedienne*
SUSAN POWTER, *fitness guru*
BETTE MIDLER, *actress*
MYLES, *lonely heart*
LAURA, *comedy writer*
GEORGE ROMAN, *Beverly Hills love psychic*
MALCOLM LEVENE, *image consultant*
BRYCE BRITTON, *sex therapist*
DEBRA WINKLER, *President,*
Personal Search Dating Agency
BARBARA DE ANGELIS,
marriage counsellor and therapist
ALEXANDRA PAUL, *actress,* Baywatch
LISA STAHL, *actress,* Baywatch Nights, a
Baywatch spin-off
DOE GENTRY, *singles correspondent*
DEAN, *gay matchmaker*
CHAD, *his client*
DAVID KULMAN, *gay matchmaker*

SHERRI SPILLANE, *scandal agent,*
who handles public relations for those who
have a good story to sell
DAN BENDER, *Internet user*
NANCY BENDER, *Dan's wife*
DR PAT ALLEN, *relationship therapist*
CARLA SINCLAIR, *Author of* Net Chick
KELLY LANGE, *Author of* Trophy Wives
OLIVIA GOLDSMITH,
author of First Wives Club
LISA SIMMONS, *journalist*
BRIDGET, *escort*
ALANA STEWART, *ex-wife of*
George Hamilton and Rod Stewart
EMILY SCOTT-LOWE, *marriage therapist*
DR GARY TAKOWSKY, *plastic surgeon*
JULIE, *Dr Takowsky's receptionist*
CINDY, *who's had vaginal enhancement*
KENNEDY, *presenter,* MTV
JULIE, *Sex Symbol Dynasty Group*
– a group of porn actresses
who work together
ELIZABETH KUSTER,
author of Exorcizing Your Ex
RUTH WEBB, *scandal agent*
EVELYN BROWN, *author*
STACY, *teenager*
FRANCIS, *teenager*
TRUE LOVE PASTOR
LOU PAGET, *creator of sexuality seminars and*
sex educator
AMANDA DE CADANET, *TV presenter*
and actress
NICK, *owner,* Mile High Ventures
GREG AND ALICE, *members,* Mile High Club
BURT WARD, *actor,* Batman and Robin
GEORGE FALARDEAU, *playboy*
DOYLE BARNETT, *couples mediator*
MARY ANNE, *sex addict*

DR ROBERT WEISS, *sexual addiction consultant*
SAMANTHA, *guest at sex party*
DENNIS FRANZ, *actor,* NYPD Blue
DIVINE BROWN, *ex-prostitute, who was arrested with Hugh Grant*
DR DAVID LEVY, *psychologist*
BRENDA LOVE, *author of* Encyclopedia of Unusual Sexual Practices
DENNIS LOWE, *marriage therapist*
NIKI STIRLING, *porn star*
NINA HARTLEY, *porn star*
SHERI, *phone sex actress*
CHERIE, *phone sex actress*
ROBERT BLOOM, *lonely heart*
DR URI PELES, *sex therapist*
CHRIS, *male escort*
SEYMORE BUTTS, *porn star*
JOHN, *erection drug user*
NAOMI, *sex charm consultant*
JEFF VALENCIA, *foot and bug fetishist, and film maker who runs Squish Productions*
KIM, *safe sex party goer*
GERALD, *guest at sex party*
TREVOR, *guest at sex party*
MONIQUE, *Sex Symbol Dynasty Group*
JOHN, *private investigator*
RHONDA, *Sex Symbol Dynasty Group*
STEVE MASON, *member and organizer,* The Lifestyles Organization, a club for swingers
GEORGE, *member,* The Lifestyles Organization
KITTY FOX, *porn star*
RICHARD, *guest at sex party*
SUKI, *sex surrogate*
BART, *Suki's client*
GOLDIE HAWN, *actress*
JULIA VERDIN, *producer*
COLIN COWIE, *wedding co-ordinator*
JENNIFER LOFTFIELD, *wedding co-ordinator*
AVRON AND LISA ANSTEY,

AVRON AND LISA ANSTEY,
who are planning their wedding
CHARLOTTE RICHARDS, *minister,*
The Little White Wedding Chapel, Vegas
KATHLEEN, *minister,* Divine Madness Fantasy
Wedding Chapel, Vegas
LINDA ESSEX, *22-times married*
JESSIE CHANDLER, *one of Linda's exes*
GLEN 'SCOTTY' WOOD, *28-times married*
SORRELL TROPE, *celebrity lawyer*
DAVID CARRADINE, *actor*
LEE METZENBAUM, *married to a younger woman*
TERRY METZENBAUM, *Lee's wife*
DOUGLAS BAGBY, *celebrity lawyer*
ARLAN, *who is 'marrying' David*
LISA, *rabbi for David and Arlan*
AMY, *Arlan's daughter*
DAVID, *who is 'marrying' Arlan*
ANDY, *guest at singles party*
JAY LENO, *chat show host*
BETTE MIDLER, *actress*
PATTI, *member,* Club 40-Something Dating Group
DIANE KEATON, *actress*
SHIRLEY LaSPINA,
who runs a group for divorced women
IAN, *partner of Alexandra Paul*
DEBRA, *private investigator*
PEGGY ESTRADA, *ex-wife of Erik Estrada, actor*
CHARLIE SHEEN, *actor*
LYN LANDON, *ex-wife of Michael Landon, actor*
DR GRAHAM, *who runs a sperm bank*

CHAPTER ONE

Dating in Hollywood

" You can have
a million girls
to do what-
ever you want
& they all look
gorgeous
JOAN RIVERS, COMEDIENNE **"**

Gena Lee Nolin, actress, *Baywatch*

INTRODUCTION

> *Hollywood isn't obsessed with sex because Hollywood is obsessed with image. If you don't have the right look, you're not in.*
>
> GEORGE ROMAN
> BEVERLY HILLS
> LOVE PSYCHIC

Dating in Hollywood is a tricky affair. It's fraught with anxieties. Are my breasts big enough? Am I slim enough? Do I drive the right car? Do I have the right zip code? Am I too old? Everything is up for scrutiny and the competition is fierce. As Joan Rivers says, 'The worst place in the world to be single is either in a convent where you'll never meet anybody, or in California if you're over 22.'

Everyone goes to extreme lengths to ensure they're in with the best possible chance. Dating agencies flourish, catering for all needs, and expectations are high.

Therapists do good business as individuals strive to establish an identity in a society that focuses on the superficial. So, too, do plastic surgeons, who will put anyone under the knife in the name of the body beautiful. From lips and tucks to vaginal enhancement - the latest treatment available for women who feel they need to look more 'youthful and mounded' in their nether regions. Nothing is best left alone, if changing it means a better chance of finding a mate.

When everyone around you is beautiful, which generally for women means looking like Barbie with a pulse and for men, having a body that shouts six hours a day in the gym, the pressure to stay in the fast lane is constant. Fall behind and you are no longer part of the magic. George Roman, a Beverly Hills love psychic, comments, 'Hollywood isn't obsessed with sex because Hollywood if obsessed with image. If you don't have the right look, you're not in.'

Image is paramount. You drive a car that speaks of money, you wear clothes that scream success. You eat, if you can possibly wangle your way in, at the currently hip restaurants and hope that you don't have to make an embarrassing scene in order to be seated at the right table. Even then you can't relax, because you can't really eat what you want. Hungry? Forget it! Eating lots in LA is not cool. You pick at delicate, fashionable food, sip juice and mineral water. Smoke at your peril.

It's stressful, it's tacky and thousands of starry eyed young hopefuls pour off the buses coming in from all over the States every year, just to be a part of it. The glamour, the money, the celebrities, the sunshine - a slice of the American dream. Tinsel town.

DATING DIFFICULTIES

STEPHANIE BEACHAM, ACTRESS:
LA is a bad place for dating. For example, a little while ago I was seated at dinner with five of the most handsome men I have ever seen in my life and not one of them was available because they were all gay. I'm a little upset about that. Yes, I think it's a very difficult place. It's difficult because, well, I call it the 'food chain culture'. You have to choose someone who is at about the same level on the food chain as you are. If you go too far down the food chain well, that's okay, but stay in, don't go out. Don't be seen with anybody who's too far down the food chain. That sucks, doesn't it? It really very silly, but that's how it is.

> *Don't be seen with anybody who's too far down the food chain. That sucks, doesn't it?*
> STEPHANIE BEACHAM

ARLENE, COMEDIENNE:
First of all you have got to ask yourself some questions. Number one, 'Is he employed?' You need a man with a job so he can buy you trinkets and things. Number two,

is he your cousin? You don't want to date a cousin - the kids come out looking funny when you do that. Number three, you have to make sure he's not one of those cop shows. You know, like America's Most Wanted or Unsolved Mysteries or any of those. You have to watch them all the time.

CHRISTINE O'KEEFE, BEVERLY HILLS MATCHMAKER:
In the '90s, the men want a woman that they can have a great conversation with but when they get her into the bedroom, she's a tiger. And they want someone very exciting and very alluring and very sexy. And someone that knows how to leave her work at work.

ROGER CLINTON, BROTHER OF BILL:
Why is it impossible to date in L.A.? I guess if I go back a few years - because I did my share! - it wasn't impossible for me and it didn't seem impossible for the people around me. But I know that there are a lot of factors that go into dating these days. I mean I am 39 and I am getting on that ladder. I know that years ago when I was at the bottom of that ladder I never had to do a background check. They didn't own me and I didn't own them... But now you want to know if their blood has been tested, the last ten people they were with. It's like you have to fill out an application. You know, who were your last five employers, who were your last five lovers, where have you been lately, who you have been with, have you had all your tests and shots. It's ridiculous. A lot of people don't want to go through all of that trouble. It can certainly be a little more difficult than it used to be.

DR RACHEL COPELAN, COUPLES COUNSELLOR AND HYPNOTHERAPIST:
Truck drivers, they're good healthy men usually. But I've known a few who wore lace underwear. Men who wear lace underwear, there are lots of them in Hollywood, it's a way of relaxing. It doesn't mean they're not good

> *I think the worst two places in the world to be single are either in a convent, where you'll never meet any men, or in California if you're over 22.*
>
> JOAN RIVERS

lovers, they're not macho guys, or anything else. It's that they're so stressed that they need something soft and tender around their butt to make them feel like a relaxed cozy child. They want to feel cuddled. So don't say no to a man who wears lacy underwear because that could be the perfect lover. I know that for a fact because a woman came in here with her boyfriend and she says, 'I really love him, he's great in bed, he does everything great, but I'm embarrassed because when he takes his trousers off he's got these black lace panties! It's sort of shocking to me!' And I said, 'Well, why don't you start wearing boxer shorts, you know? Kind of balance the look?' And that's what she did and they developed a wonderful thing. They're getting married as a matter of fact.

DIANE CONWAY, COMEDIENNE AND FAIRY GODMOTHER: If you fall in love with a facade, one day the facade's going to slip, no matter how many times you get those

People here are way too superficial and 50% of all marriages in California end in a divorce.

DIANE CONWAY

eyes lifted. People here are way too superficial and 50% of all marriages in California end in a divorce. I mean that's high. And the reason it's hard is they've been hurt. People are like prickly little cactuses, they're afraid to be approached. They're very gun shy.

JOAN RIVERS:

Well, I have to be careful of men. First of all, the men I go out with are so old! I have one man, he gave me a hickey and left his teeth in my neck. I met another man - a very rich Greek - but he had a urinary problem. I used to call him the leaking tanker.

I think the worst two places in the world to be single are either in a convent, where you'll never meet any men, or in California if you're over 22.

JACKIE COLLINS, AUTHOR:

Smart women don't jump into bed with a man because you know it's so available that way.

RITA RUDNER, COMEDIENNE:

LA especially is very, everyone's so self-centred, so a date in LA would be like a person sitting there going how do I look to you now, or do I still look good, do I need surgery yet, is anything wrinkling?

DIANE CONWAY:

I have appointed myself the fairy godmother of dating and mating for love and romance. I am very well qualified because I have dated every dysfunctional man in America and a few in England and Europe and I still found my prince. This time it's the fairy godmother who got the prince! I have a successful loving relationship so I know what I'm talking about. All you need is one.

I wrote a book called *The Fairy Godmother Guide to Dating and Mating* because I think that people need hope, and especially humour, when it comes to relationships. Relationships can be so tedious, people don't get along, then all this weird stuff happens and you end up with the wrong person.

You want to make sure the man does not have a criminal record, is not on America's Most Wanted, things like that.

You want to check a man out and make sure he has the qualities that you want. For instance, right at the top of my list was humour. I am a funny person and I want to be with a funny person. I want to laugh and have fun. I also wanted loyalty, honesty and monogamy, and that's a word that most men do not even know how to spell! You have to be very careful with these. Get yourself a DNA testing kit, so when they come home at night you can do a little testing on their underwear to see where they've been. Then you just have to nip that right in the bud. Oh yeah, you have to take a firm hand with these things!

You should absolutely not have sex on the first date. Absolutely not! There aren't enough condoms in the world. You have to get that man to jump through hoops - like a dog. Having sex on the first date is a terrible idea

> *You have to get that man to jump through hoops – like a dog.*
> DIANE CONWAY

because you have to get to know somebody a little bit first. That's anonymous sex, it's not good for you. You're going to end up feeling shallow. No, no, no, don't do it! Bad girl, bad girl!

Your Fairy Godmother has a little message for you: if you haven't seen a man and he hasn't called in about three weeks, if you're in doubt about the whereabouts of a man, chances are he is not in the emergency room moaning your name. He is probably onto a new conquest, watching TV, channel surfing. Move on, because you could miss the real love of your life waiting for Mr. Nitwit who hasn't called in three weeks.

FLIRTING

DENISE GILBERT, MISS FLIRT USA

The way you dress and present yourself are very important when you're flirting and looking for a man. My personal flirting tips would be: love yourself and get into yourself. I know that sounds egotistical and self-righteous but only when you really, truly love yourself can you love other people.

I've heard some real bad pick-up lines, like 'We're having a party over at my house after this, you want to come over?' Like I really want to go over to their house at two in the morning and party some more - I don't think so! Another bad line is: "I have this great stereo system in my car, want to come check it out?" Oh yeah, like I really want to go out in the parking lot with you and check out your car stereo!

> *The way you dress and the way you present yourself are very important when you're flirting.*
>
> DENISE GILBERT

RICHARD GOSS, CHAIRMAN OF AMERICAN SINGLES
American Singles is the second-largest singles organization in the world. We organize events like the Black and White Ball all over the country.

It should be easy to find a date in America because there are 73 million single people to choose from. The problem is everybody is chicken. Everybody wants the other person to put their ego on the line and make the first move. So everyone plays hard to get and everybody winds up staying home and complaining that they never meet anybody.

I teach flirting classes and I teach people that flirting is easy in just three little steps. Number one is eye contact - you have to stare at people; number two, give them a big smile; and number three, say something. That's it. You know, they did this study in LA. They asked all the single people what their best opening line was. You know what they said? 'Hi'. You don't have to be clever, you don't have to be original. You don't even have to be funny. All you have to do is put your ego on the line, take a deep breath, and say 'Hi'. This is not brain surgery, it is real simple! Anybody can do it. In fact babies are natural flirts. You notice babies are not afraid of rejection. They smile at everybody and everybody falls in love with them. The same is true with singles. If you're an adult single and you say 'Hi' to people, smile and make eye contact, you can't help but be a successful flirt.

CHRISTINE O'KEEFE:
How do I teach my clients to flirt? It amazes me how many people don't know how to flirt. People think they know how to flirt. They think that if they just make eye contact for a second that's enough.

I have to teach my clients by role playing. I have to play their part and they play my part and we have little role plays in my office before they leave. If that's an area that they are very underdeveloped in, I show them little techniques. Oh, they all laugh and blush and they think

It's a game. Smart ladies know that, the Jaqueline Onassises' of the world knew that. I watch them in action and these ladies know how to flirt.

JOAN RIVERS

it's hysterical but part of it is to encourage them to go and do it right away before they chicken out.

PHYLLIS DILLER, COMEDIENNE:
Flirting? Look, if you don't know how to flirt, there is no hope. Besides, if you learn it and try it, it will be phoney. I mean if you flutter your eyelashes it would look so dumb it would frighten people away.

SUSAN POWTER, FITNESS GURU:
Flirting tips coming from an ex-stripper? Hmm. I think the best way to flirt is to be comfortable with your own sensuality - to reek sensuality not sex - whether it is in a movement, a look or a gesture.

That to me is the ultimate in flirting and within that there is a very broad range. I mean, you could do hand signals. You could do eye movements, use body language. But I don't think you could do any of it effectively or beautifully unless you are really comfortable with your sensuality. And women are just fabulous. We have breasts. We have bellies. God, what is prettier than a naked woman? I mean, really, look at naked men! You know, you have to love somebody to like their penis. You can't just love any penis. I mean they're really ugly! But women are beautiful.

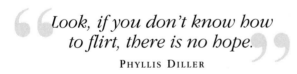

Look, if you don't know how to flirt, there is no hope.
PHYLLIS DILLER

STEPHANIE BEACHAM:
I have no flirting skills whatsoever. I only have, 'Don't come within a hundred yards of me and if you think you're gonna talk to me, please change your mind'. I don't have flirting skills. I don't think dropping hankies works anymore? Does it? I have no idea, no idea. I interview people. I'm ruthless. I'm so horrid. Flirting skills? No! Ask somebody else.

IMAGE

BETTE MIDLER, ACTRESS:
You have to look a certain way, you have to have this man, you have to have this car, it's terrible!

CHRISTINE O'KEEFE:
People get so caught up with the image of having the right dress, being seen in the right restaurant, driving the right car, living in the right neighborhood, having the right zip code. I mean it's that silly! Some area codes are just not cool and others are great.

MYLES, LONELY HEART:
I once dated a woman who lived in this apartment building that was, by LA standards, considered geographically undesirable. The building itself was nice, but being in a drug-infested run-down part of Hollywood made this very unpleasant trip late at night just for sex.

LAURA, COMEDY WRITER:
It's a very trendy town. You can meet someone and be their best friend for two months. Then you don't hear from them for a week and you find out they moved back to Australia or they went back to New York or they're dead. Or all of the above.

GEORGE ROMAN, BEVERLY HILLS LOVE PSYCHIC:
Hollywood isn't obsessed with sex because Hollywood is obsessed with image. If you don't have the right look, you're not in.

PHYLLIS DILLER:
An image consultant? Well you should study your own self and 'to thine own self be true'. In other words, find out what is best for you and stick with it. A fat lady shouldn't wear pants. I mean, when you are following a fat lady

A fat lady shouldn't wear pants. I mean, it shouldn't look like two small boys fighting under a blanket.

PHYLLIS DILLER

> *I've met a
> ton of women
> who hate
> being fat.
> I've been fat.
> It does not
> look or
> feel good.
> Naked fat is
> not cute.*

SUSAN POWTER

down the street, and she has got pants on, it shouldn't look like two small boys fighting under a blanket.

MALCOLM LEVENE, IMAGE CONSULTANT:
We need communication skills, we need a good smile, we need to be present and make eye contact, we need to stay with the program, we need to have our shoulders

> *I wonder how much plastic surgery one can have before you lose something of who you are.*
> MALCOLM LEVENE

relaxed and our feet positioned in a way that makes us feel grounded. These are the fundamentals of good style. These are the things that we loved about Audrey Hepburn and Cary Grant. They just knew what to do.

But if we think about the present, we have Andie MacDowell and Diane Keaton. Even Bruce Willis, in a way, because he's so funny and self-effacing and he doesn't care that he's losing his hair. He doesn't care that he doesn't get credited for every role that he plays. It's courage that speaks of style. Courage of your convictions to know who you are. I mean to walk around with a polka-dot rag on your head and go to a premiere looking almost trashy, takes a lot of courage, but Bruce still does it.

Speaking about Demi [Moore], I wonder how much plastic surgery one can have before you lose something of who you really are. I mean from what I understand, if the gossip is true (and it's just great gossip even if it's not true) she's had everything done except her toes, and they're next on the list. I just wonder what that says about who you are and what is left of you when you've just given everything away or had everything done.

Sharon Stone is the best, I mean she is just so wicked, isn't she? Apparently at the last Oscars she and her shoulders arrived and they did a fantastic job. But what was wonderful was her little black dress that everybody thought cost $7000. It was actually a black top from The Gap and $19.95. Great style, great style.

BRYCE BRITTON, SEX THERAPIST:
I would say that the individuals in Los Angeles have a lot of problems around their body image and that impacts on their sexuality. And it's because we're constantly comparing ourself with the media standard.

> *we want bigger breasts or a bigger butt or more plastic surgery or a bigger penis... the emphasis here is very external*
>
> BRYCE BRITTON

We're constantly comparing our cars and the way we look and what diet we're on. And we want bigger breasts or a bigger butt or more plastic surgery or a bigger penis. So I think the emphasis here is very external and people forget about what's happening inside. They become split. They present themselves as being totally accomplished and feeling great and looking wonderful and inside they're scared. They're performing like crazy. They're disconnected and unhappy. But there are a lot of people who are beautiful, happy and connected and have it all.

DEBRA WINKLER, PRESIDENT, PERSONAL SEARCH DATING AGENCY:
Here everybody comes from somewhere else. Nobody is accountable. That's why you get this kind of flakey behaviour in Los Angeles because there is no-one in that close family circle to say, 'Don't behave that way.'

The more we feel we have to be perfect on the outside the more we're covering up how imperfect we feel on the inside.

BARBARA DE ANGELIS

BARBARA DE ANGELIS,
MARRIAGE COUNSELLOR AND THERAPIST:
There's something interesting happening with the idea of image in Hollywood. One is the traditional trend where image is everything, you have to be perfect, you have to have plastic surgery, you have to look 20, you have to weigh nothing and have no cellulite, your skin has to be perfect, you have to have the perfect new clothes and so on. And that still goes on, it's evident when you look at fashion magazines and when you go to openings. But then there is what I call an intelligent backlash that's been happening in the last seven years. One example is Rosie O'Donnell who has a new talk show. She is somewhat overweight and she's just not dieting or trying to look any different. Another is Susan Sarandon who is going on camera and making films with no make-up and saying, 'I'm over 40 and have several children and this is how I look.' It's a different kind of beauty. It's intelligent because beauty has very little to do with what's on the outside. It has to do with someone's soul and their heart. So although you still have *Baywatch* and *Melrose Place* I think you are seeing that people, especially as they mature, are not buying into all that anymore, they're not trying to look 20 when they're 40. They're saying, 'This is me, I'm mature, I'm beautiful, take it or leave it'.

People who have an obsession with how they look or with the way they are sexually have usually experienced a lot of emotional damage in childhood. They've never formed a strong sense of self-love, they've experienced a lot of rejection when they were quite young and are desperate to feel good, to feel worthy, to feel accepted and so they translate those inner desires into outer desires, 'I want to look good, I want to be accepted physically for how I am', because secretly inside they feel so damaged. The more we feel we have to be perfect on the outside the more we're covering up how imperfect we really feel on the inside.

ALEXANDRA PAUL, ACTRESS, *BAYWATCH*:

I guess I think that *Baywatch* does project a certain image of what is attractive. The women are slender. For the most part they're curvaceous - except for me! The guys are muscular and mostly white. But there are also some very good images. For example, the character played by David Hasselhoff is a very responsible single father who loves his son. And it portrays women in good jobs, equal to men, doing very physical things, saving people. That's a heroic image.

You know what? In America, women are taught that having a big appetite is unfeminine. A big appetite for food. A big appetite for sex. A big appetite for anything. If you want too much of anything, that's not feminine.

SUSAN POWTER:

Image in Hollywood? I don't think image in Hollywood is any more important than image anywhere else. I mean

"Women really love a Ferrari or a convertible.

JACKIE COLLINS

image on Wall Street and on Madison Avenue is pretty important. I think our society, especially where women are concerned, is very much based on image. I don't really know if that's bad or good, I think it depends on who you are.

I've met a ton of women who hate being fat. I've been fat. It does not look or feel good, I can promise you. Naked fat is not cute.

LISA STAHL, ACTRESS, *BAYWATCH NIGHTS*:
I have a very nice car that I cannot afford - it is killing me! But it is such an ego boost to drive down Sunset Boulevard in my black Porsche and my hair is flying and the guys are whistling. I love it! I can't help it.

I think this obsession with image started with Barbie dolls way back then. What do they say? If Barbie were a human she'd be 6'2" and have a waist of thirteen inches or something preposterous.

JOAN RIVERS:

In California everyone goes to every length to look good and the exercising is insane. They don't go to the gym for an hour. They go to the gym for five hours, for six hours. The emphasis is on the body. The emphasis is on the latest thing in liposuction and plastic surgery and hair transplants. Everything to look good and there is such a strain on these people. And the sad thing is, they all look alike. You walk into Mortans, and there will be a thousand short guys with cigars and a thousand tall blondes, all of whom are gorgeous. Or you will see a thousand rich older female stars with these happy boys sitting next to them. I've watched a lot of men in California going from one star to another. They make their living by being companions to female stars and, then, if they are lucky, and one of them was very, very lucky, they end up with an extremely rich star who then dies.

DATING AGENCIES

JOAN RIVERS:

Today men expect women to sleep with them on the first date. The 'sleeping with someone' becomes an automatic thing. You sleep with someone, and then find out if you are compatible. I just find the whole thing so distasteful. I also find that women have lost the control. And I find it so obnoxious that now it's the men, men, who can't commit, and you find forty-five year old men saying that they're not ready for marriage. No, you're not, you are ready for death!

SUSAN POWTER:

Dating agencies? Well, I have a very dear friend, she is one of the brightest women I've ever met, I love her, and she has a lovely relationship with her husband. They have two children together, and they have a passionate thing going on. But when she told me that she met him

> *In California everyone goes to every length to look good and the exercising is insane. They don't go to the gym for an hour. They go to the gym for five hours, for six hours.*
>
> JOAN RIVERS

through a dating service, for a moment I lost all respect for her. I said, 'Lisa, what the hell is the matter with you? What are you, nuts?' But when she explained the system to me, I was fascinated. I mean, she listed what she wanted so there's a great elimination process. It's kind of like a good bowel movement, you know, there is an immediate elimination. You can screen them all beforehand so, you know, so even if they've got all the core essentials, if they are dog ugly, you can see and decide whether you are interested or not. I think it is an okay way to date. But I wouldn't do it because, you know, if I'm going to pay $15,000 I want a different man every night, for 15 nights. You know what I am saying? I mean a thousand bucks a night! For that, I'm going to want massive sex. But she did it, and she's happy.

DOE GENTRY, SINGLES CORRESPONDENT:
I think dating agencies are good because people are very busy in their lives and they don't have time to go out looking for somebody. However, some agencies play on people's emotions and rip them off financially. Because singles are very vulnerable, they're always being rejected or rejecting and that leaves them in a very peculiar spot. And in LA when you meet somebody you always wonder what they want. It's not, 'Are they attracted to me?' It's, 'I wonder what they want from me?'

> *in LA when you meet somebody...*
> *it's not, 'Are they attracted to me?' it's*
> *'I wonder what they want from me?'*
> **DOE GENTRY**

At a gay video dating agency, Dean, gay matchmaker, is making a video of Chad, his client, to go on the files:
Dean: So, what I want to know, if you were any part of a farm, anything associated with a farm, what would you be?

> *You can screen them all beforehand so, you know, so even if they've got all the core essentials, if they are dog ugly, you can see and decide whether you are interested or not.*
>
> SUSAN POWTER

Chad: Probably Babe.

Dean: Babe?

Chad: Babe.

Dean: The talking pig?

Chad: Yes.

Dean: Because?

Chad: I don't know. I loved the movie, I thought it was really cute. But there was something about the characterization of the pig that was just so sweet and, on a farm, that's the only thing I could imagine being.

Dean: But you have a mom, right?

Chad: Yeah, I do have a mom.

DAVID KULMAN, GAY MATCHMAKER:

Okay. And he likes travel, theatre, opera, ballet, all that. And swimming, jet skiing, the gym of course. Everybody goes to the gym. The beach, walking. And he wants someone thirty to forty-five. And you're sexually matched because as I've told you before Wally, you can't match two anal passives. And he prefers someone who's not hairy. He's a little hairy and you're not hairy. It seems like a good match. You might like him. And you can call him between 6:00 and 10:30 p.m. Monday through Friday and 10:00 a.m. to 10:30 p.m. Saturday and Sunday. Oh, and he's got two cats. But you're not allergic, so that's okay and you want a cat. And no, he's never been married unlike you, you know. But he doesn't mind children, and you have two kids. And since they're teenagers, they can come and visit you both.

DEBRA WINKLER:

A good question that I ask at the seminars I hold is this: I ask the gentlemen what they think the proper time is to wait before calling a lady they met at a party. They all say between three and five days. Then I ask the ladies when they would like to be called. And they all say they would like to be called the next morning. I call this the difference between boy time and girl time. For girls, even waiting 24 hours is a very long time, so by the time the guy calls five days later, they are mad.

> *For girls, even waiting 24 hours is a very long time, so by the time the guy calls five days later, they are mad.*
> DEBRA WINKLER

LISA STAHL:

I've seen so many talk shows about people who have consulted dating services and met guys from the personal columns. I think it's a very scary thing, I would never do that. You might end up with some murderer or some guy who is kinky or something.

CHRISTINE O'KEEFE:

Before they come in for an interview, I advise people to

A date in Beverly Hills

write down their non-negotiable and negotiable qualities like being honest, trustworthy, loyal, articulate, intelligent, having a good sense of integrity. These are all non-negotiables in my opinion and they really should be on

> *They probably had Mr or Miss Right in their grasp at one point in their life and they didn't even notice.*
>
> CHRISTINE O'KEEFE

everyone's checklist.

I get them to do checklists and I go through them with them so they can see where there's a huge dichotomy. If a woman asks for a man who's sensitive and loving and compassionate and strong and dynamic and professional, I say, 'Did you want two for the price of one or just the one?' Most of the time all these qualities don't mix. What we have to do is go through the list and determine which ones are vitally important and which aren't.

And we get to the core of the matter, right there in that one simple little exercise, but most people have never done it. It's why their relationships have failed. They probably had Mr or Miss Right in their grasp at one point in their life and they didn't ever notice.

DEBRA WINKLER:

I work with a lot of well-known people, especially in my Beverly Hills office. Sometimes you get really unusual requests. I had one Mormon gentleman and he not only wanted a woman who was Morman but she had to be a ballerina too. There are probably only about two in the whole world! So I started in Salt Lake City where most of the Mormons live. That's what I call a real special search.

We did find a source that listed every professional ballet company in the world so I wrote a letter to them explaining who my client was, why he was interested, and asked if there was anybody that met my gentleman friend's requirements and wanted to meet him.

The more specific a request the client makes, the harder it is to find people and so the more expensive it becomes. It is very expensive for the special searches, between $10,000 and $20,000.

DAVID KULMAN:

If you put an ad in the paper, I mean, who's gonna say they're short, fat, poor and ugly? You know, they're all wonderful in the paper.

Truck drivers, they're good healthy men usually. But I've known a few who wore lace underwear. Men who wear lace underwear, there are lots of them in Hollywood, its a way of relaxing. It doesn't mean they're not good lovers, they're not macho guys, or anything else. It's that they're so stressed that they need something soft and tender around their butt to make them feel like a relaxed cozy child. They want to feel cuddled. So don't say no to a man who wears lacy underwear because that could be the perfect lover. I know that for a fact because a women came in here with her boyfriend and she says, 'I really love him, he's great in bed, he does everything great, but I'm embarrassed because when he takes his trousers off he's got on these black lace panties! It's sort of shocking to me!' And I said to her, 'Well, why don't you start wearing boxer shorts, you know? To kind of balance the look?' And so that's what she did and they developed a really wonderful thing. They're getting married soon as a matter of fact.

> *I would rather spend the night with my cocker spaniel than some person from a dating service. I think it's very degrading.*
>
> SHERRI SPILLANE, SCANDAL AGENT

> *If you put an ad in the paper, I mean, who's gonna say they're short, fat, poor and ugly?*
>
> DAVID KULMAN

INTERNET DATING

> *People are willing to say much more about themselves over the Internet than they would if they were meeting someone in person.*
>
> DAN BENDER

DAN BENDER, INTERNET USER:
People are much more relaxed when they communicate through a computer, they open up. It's not face to face so they don't feel like they're going to get rejected or people are going to make up their minds about them. And so it works out very well. People are willing to say much more about themselves over the Internet than they would if they were meeting someone in person.

The Internet can be very sexy. When two people start communicating they keep on building, building and before you know it they're throwing out sexual innuendos here and there. What would you do if this? What would you do if that? And it can be very enticing.

NANCY BENDER, DAN'S WIFE:
The Internet can definitely be sexy. It has that mystery to it. You don't know the person and you're talking. And you could talk sexy to a person up to a point.

My first reaction when I met Dan was kind of embarrassing, it was nice. I was glad to finally meet him because I knew all about this person and it was like we were old friends, sitting down and talking.

Then after nine months of romance, we got married.

DAN BENDER:
Which resulted in having 17-month old Noah here. So I would highly recommend it.

DR PAT ALLEN, RELATIONSHIP THERAPIST:
The Internet is a great place to have fantasy relationships, but until you meet the human being it's not real. Chemistry is taste, touch, smell, seeing and hearing - you don't read chemistry, you see it. So it's a nice place to fantasize, but it's not really somewhere to meet someone on the basis of chemistry, which is the foundation of any relationship.

CARLA SINCLAIR, AUTHOR OF *NET CHICK*:

I think it's dangerous to date on the Internet if you take it too seriously before you actually meet the person in person. I think that people should be aware that when you're on the Internet, you obviously don't really know who's on the other side of the conversation. There have been instances where young girls have been on line, met a boy and fall head over heels with them. All they're seeing are words. They're not seeing the other person. They don't know what the other person looks like. And I have heard of cases where a girl goes and meets a boy she's met on the Internet but actually the boy's a man and the man supposedly rapes the girl. But I think that that's just foolishness on the girl's part. She shouldn't

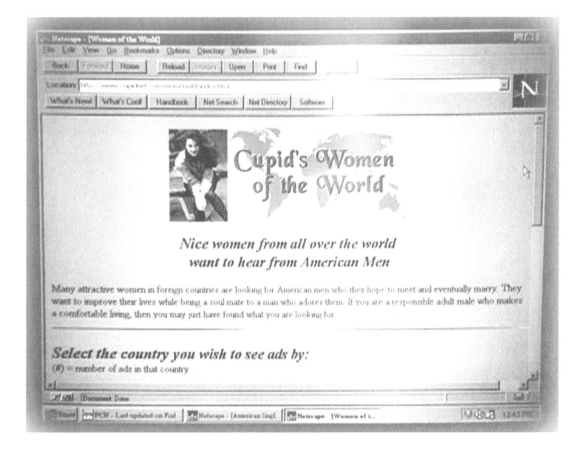

have met him in a hotel room or at his house. She should have met him at a restaurant or somewhere public.

> *All they're seeing are words.*
> *They're not seeing the other person.*
> CARLA SINCLAIR

SUSAN POWTER:

Well, I happen to think the Internet is a fabulous medium. Bill Gates is my hero. I worship him, and if you could infuse an ounce of personality into the man I think that he would be the second coming. The man is great. It is an incredible, explosive medium. Unfortunately, like television it is being abused. Because, I mean, there's nothing but sex chat lines, and they're so juvenile and stupid. It's a pity the medium isn't being used for communication internationally. I mean it is but, you know, on such a nothing level. But it will build to that. But I think that the disadvantage is that these sex lines on the Internet are kind of like phone sex. You know, you can have these conversations and be anything you want to be, and then when you meet the person, they are like 800 pounds on a good day and you know that is why they are on-line. I mean, you know, 'Yeah, I'm Bill and my penis is this big'. And when you meet him, and he is two feet tall and two feet long, if you know what I mean. I'm on the Internet myself. I don't bother chatting because I haven't found anything worth chatting about yet.

> *Well, it's a good thing because*
> *it's very difficult to catch a disease.*
> *But it's also dangerous because, you know,*
> *people do lie and you could be dating*
> *your brother.*
> RITA RUDNER

> *...they are like 800 pounds on a good day and you know that is why they are on-line.*
>
> SUSAN POWTER

PLASTIC SURGERY

DENISE GILBERT:

I think plastic surgery is great. I would love to get some work done. If you have the money, I believe you should go for it. There's nothing wrong with wearing lipstick and mascara, there's nothing wrong with going on a diet and there's definitely nothing wrong with plastic surgery. It makes you feel better about who you are and you're happier. All power to you.

I would like my nose just a little smaller. I'd like my face resurfaced for smoother skin and I'd like my lips enhanced a bit. I would love to be on the front of *Cosmopolitan* magazine but I need a little work from the doctor first.

KELLY LANGE, AUTHOR OF *TROPHY WIVES*
AND BROADCASTER:

Vaginal enhancement? I'll have to find out about that. I had no idea. I did know about vaginal tightening to make it tighter, but not vaginal enhancement. Oh, my!

OLIVIA GOLDSMITH, AUTHOR OF *FIRST WIVES CLUB*:

Plastic surgery in Hollywood in the '90s? One of the lines from *First Wives Club* where Goldie Hawn says, 'Well yes, I've been freshened.' It's like good hygiene, you know? You brush your teeth and you have surgery.

> *Oh, women will go to any length to get a date if they're lonely and needy... they will go to plastic surgeons.*
>
> SHERRI SPILLANE

SHERRI SPILLANE:

Oh, women will go to any length to get a date if they're lonely and needy. If they're unsure of themselves they

> *I've seen one woman who went to have her breasts changed three or four times. They kept getting bigger and bigger and bigger.*

SHERRI SPILLANE

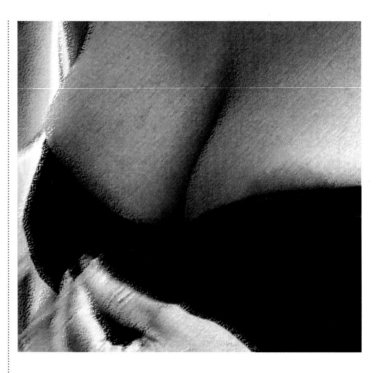

will go to plastic surgeons. I know a woman who's been to a plastic surgeon at least six or seven times since I've known her and there are some women who go more than that. I've seen one women who went to have her breasts changed three or four times. They kept getting bigger and bigger and bigger. Obviously, the men she was going with wanted that, or she thought they did. They have their buttocks done, they have their lips filled. If it makes them happy, let them do it. I wouldn't do it for a man, I would do it for myself. I have done it for myself, and I would do it again.

Fat injected in the vagina? I'm floored, I'm totally floored. I've heard of it in the lips, in the other set of lips, but never there. I don't quite understand that. Who are these people and why are they doing that? Is it some new fad? Isn't it bad enough that they're doing it with men's penises now? Look what happened to John Wayne Bobbit, he's a mess. I think there are some things that should be left alone and maybe that's one of them.

LISA SIMMONS, JOURNALIST:

People go to real extremes here to keep up their appearance. This is tinsel town after all. I mean, if someone's stupid enough they'll do anything. Like me, going and getting a $200 haircut because I heard this woman did Meg Ryan's hair and I wanted the same haircut. So I show up, I sit down and this woman's not very pleasant or polite - actually she's quite nasty. She sort of flips through my hair and says, 'Well, Meg and Julia have bushy hair too.'

Plastic surgery here is an art form. You've got cheek bone implants, lip implants, chin implants, forehead lifts. Every kind of thing you can imagine doing to your face. Breast implants, pec implants. I've even heard of penile implants. People will do a lot of things to make sure that they're good looking enough for the LA population.

BRIDGET, ESCORT:

I belong to a private gym and I think I'm the only woman there who has real breasts, you know. People call it silicone city. Everybody is very pressured - women to do aerobics and lift weights, be thin and dress the part and look great. It's very hard. And, you know, I'm in my late 20s and I already feel old in this city. There are girls here and they've just arrived from all over and they're 17, 18, 19 and men want young women. You know, after 30 they don't want you anymore. So, there's a lot of pressure to look younger, stay in shape and there's a lot of cosmetic surgery carried out to do that.

JOAN RIVERS:

You can have a million girls that are willing to sit up, lie down, bend over, stretch, do whatever you want and they all look gorgeous.

ALANA STEWART, EX-WIFE OF
GEORGE HAMILTON AND ROD STEWART:

I had breast implants put in years ago which resulted in a lot of health problems. In the end I had them removed.

JACKIE COLLINS:
There's one famous movie star who buys his girlfriends breasts. I mean, every time he goes out with them he'll say, 'You know, honey, you're a beautfiul girl but wouldn't you like a little more upstairs?'

EMILY SCOTT-LOWE, MARRIAGE THERAPIST:
For females in America, image is very important. The problems you see here - poor body image and eating disorders, particularly among young middle class and upper class women - are awful. They have really bought into the images. I grew up with TV images but now have video graphics and virtual reality. We are a very visual culture and I think technology has certainly contributed to that. We have become so image-oriented. Women are dying from it - they are dying from eating disorders because of some of these images.

DR GARY TAKOWSKY, PLASTIC SURGEON:
My practice in Beverly Hills is limited to cosmetic and reconstructive surgery and that includes procedures from head to toe. The most common type is liposuction but I also do vaginal enhancement. People who want to have this done fall into three different categories: those people who are over forty, have had children and have atrophy of the lateral walls of their labia and the external genitalia. These people want their external genitalia plumped up, more youthful looking. They also want a tighter feeling so that when they have intercourse, so they don't feel their anatomy is too wide open. The second category of women is those with a congenital abnormality. For example, some women have a small labia majora on one side and a non-existent one on the other. And fat grafting will plump up the labia to make it more symmetrical. The third category are those patients who are just average but want to look sexier and more appealing to men. They want this grafting just so they feel they have an edge on the next individual.

> *Now they're trying to convince us*
> *even our pussies aren't good enough?*
> *Get away from me.*
> *What are you, crazy?*
>
> OLIVIA GOLDSMITH

DR GARY TAKOWSKY:

The surgery is performed by extrapolating fat from different areas of the body and then emulsifying that fat so that it's usable and can pass through a 14-gauge syringe. The syringe is then placed just under the skin of the external genitalia, the labia majora, and with pressure, the syringe squirts fat into each labia majora. The process is repeated again so that there's a total of 40 ccs in each labia majora. Following that, the legs are closed and all of the fat is squished out from the labia majora into the internal lining of the vagina.

This procedure was first performed by Hilda Felicio, a plastic surgeon in Brazil, and she did it to beautify the external genitalia. Following her procedure, I realized that I could add more fat and then squish it all out and the labia looked better right away. Then I noticed that the patients were coming in and telling me that they noticed a tremendous improvement in the duration and intensity of orgasm.

SUSAN POWTER:

Why would you want large vaginal lips? For what? It's just another way of making money off of women. You know, there's nothing I like more than a doctor telling me that him doing something to me is gonna make me more feminine.

DR GARY TAKOWSKY:

The whole procedure costs about $3000 and takes from about an hour, to an hour and 15 minutes. I've patented

> *patients... want to look sexier and more appealing to men. They want this grafting just so they feel they have an edge over the next individual.*
>
> DR GARY TAKOWSKY

this procedure for the United States and for rest of the world because I thought it was going to be quite amazing.

JULIE, DR TAKOWSKY'S RECEPTIONIST:
The women who benefit the most are people who have had the same partner for a while. They're the ones who really notice the difference. But if you have different partners, it's going to be a different experience every time anyway.

We had one lady come in and her husband told her it was the best Christmas gift she could have given him. Another lady's husband told her, 'It's like being with a whole different woman'.

CINDY, WHO'S HAD VAGINAL ENHANCEMENT:
It is imperative that you're perfect. As you get older the desire to stay perfect becomes so much greater. And there are a million pretty girls out here. Millions of them, you know. I had it done purely for looks and for my own confidence. I mean, you know, bottom line, it's not really for anyone else. I don't think anybody should have any kind of surgery for anybody else. I think you have to do it for yourself.

Having the surgery will enhance my sex life because I will definitely be more confident when I take all my clothes off. And I think that that's important for anybody's sex life.

KENNEDY, PRESENTER, MTV:
Who the hell is that vain that they would have to get fat injected into their cha cha?

PHYLLIS DILLER:
Actually plastic surgery is great. Supposing you've got a terribly ugly nose or your ears need pinning because they are sticking out, or you have a hair lip. My God, they do wonderful work. Plastic surgery provides a

It's imperative that you're perfect. As you get older the desire to stay perfect becomes so much greater.

CINDY

wonderful service. But when people start to have surgery very young because they want a certain nose, or they want to look like so and so, that's when it starts to become a problem.

I can't believe that people are having surgery on their nether regions, their front nether regions, for looks because I always turn the lights out! That's why my honeymoon was such a mess. I turned the lights out and he was afraid of the dark.

But all this surgery, it's barbaric. In fact the boob jobs have got way out of hand. I worked on this video with the prettiest young girl the other day and she has the most beautiful, petite little figure and these huge jugs. I was just horrified, they are really ugly. When she gets older she is going to find out what happens to jugs that big - boy oh boy she won't want them! Then she'll have them taken off, I suppose. And then there's Dolly Parton – I worked with her too recently. Same deal: tiny little waist and these huge balloons. Poor thing! I think she had them made too, I'm sure they aren't real.

STEPHANIE BEACHAM:

I think that if you have your face lifted to the extent that your smile is permanent, it can really limit quite a few real life occasions. And I do think it's a shame when people can't keep a straight face at a funeral. I mean I think that's the case with Nancy Reagan, don't you? She can go out in public, but not to a funeral. She can't wipe the smile off her face. It's a good thing I'm not a Republican. Plastic surgery? I don't know, I'm sure it's got its place. Anything that's going to make you feel better, as long as it's really going to make you feel better, maybe you should go for it. But if it's just because you're feeling insecure, why not just deal with the insecurity?

JOAN RIVERS:

I think everyone should go to every length to look good. I don't mean keeping young, I mean looking good.

Imagine two people walk in. One is great looking. One is a piggo. You are always going to talk to the good looking one, it's human nature. Rumour has it Prince Charles had his ears pinned back. I think a doctor thinned Princess Di's nose, but not by much, because she still has to look like herself. Everybody wants to look good whoever they are and especially in California where the competition is so incredible. But I feel it can go too far. We're going to end up with a country full of women that look like they've been through the wind tunnel. And you can only do that so much 'cause pretty soon your nose is going to be touching your ears and your mouth gets really big and your teeth looks like horse's teeth. Women should not have too much plastic surgery.

SUSAN POWTER:

All these men that criticize women and breast augmentation, let me tell you something: if you could go in and get any size, perfect penis of your dreams, who wouldn't volunteer, and what would you all ask for? The biggest size available please, something thick and long.

> *I think God made plastic surgeons. God gave us this intelligent concept. Use it if you can.*
>
> JOAN RIVERS

FACE READING

GEORGE ROMAN:

For the past 15 years I've helped people from all over the world with their relationships. I believe that everybody has psychic intuitive powers, I've just developed mine.

People consult me on face reading or personalogy. Face reading basically looks at the structure of the face and the body and how you respond to others based on that structure. In a relationship it's very important that the couple have similarities in certain key areas, like their chins.

Demi Moore and Bruce Willis:

Now let's look at the compatibility between Bruce Willis and Demi Moore. There are three different areas to examine: the first is the physical area which is the most important for sexual attraction and sex drive. And I can see that the physical attraction is not very strong. Maybe initially in the relationship there was an attraction, but in the long term, physical attraction is not the real reason why they got together. Their emotional compatibility is only 57 per cent, which is kind of in the medium range. That means that they might stay together or they might not could maybe stay together, it's in that 50-50 range.

Probably they did come together for emotional reasons, rather than physical and intellectual ones which are very low. So they definitely did not come together for their ability to communicate with each other because they don't relate to each other intellectually. This doesn't have anything to do with IQ, don't interpret it as one being smarter than the other. It has more to do with their reasoning and communicative abilities, the ability to relate to each other mentally and intellectually. Similar beliefs, you could say. But with 33 per cent they have very little in common on that level. So it seems the only reason why they are together is this emotional reading of 57 per

> *If they give up the relation-ship, it'll be her choice, not Bruce's. She'll make the first step to break it or end it.*

GEORGE ROMAN

cent, which leads me to believe that, in the long run, this relationship will not last.

As far as their faces are concerned, Demi Moore has a very broad face and this reflects her high confidence. People with broad faces tend to 'fake it 'till they make it', which is very good if you're an actress. She can take on many different roles and come across like she's the real thing. She's also got a wide jaw line which indicates authority. She likes to take charge, she likes to take control of situations. And she's also got arched eyebrows signifying a love of drama and the performing arts.

Bruce Willis, however, has a thinner face, which means that his confidence is gained through knowledge and information, that he's not born with natural confidence like Demi. He has had to learn to be confident. The more he knows, the more confident he feels. With his facial expression, his eyebrows are not as arched as Demi's, which means that Bruce has some appreciation of drama, but not as much as Demi, so there's a little bit of a difference there, but they do have a dramatic appreciation in common.

They both have angular, wedge-shaped chins, so they are both argumentative and stubborn. It's fine for both of them to have it, but if one of them had a more rounded chin, that person would feel bullied or picked on by the angular-chinned person. They both have ears that are set apart from their head, indicating that they are people who like to possess, own or control. Demi's are far out, similar to Ross Perot's ears, which basically indicates that she has a very strong need to possess, own or control things or people. And that's good for accumulating wealth and for keeping a relationship.

I would say that if this relationship was to break up, which I think it will in the long term, she will end it, not Bruce. Because she has the stronger tendency towards for authoritativeness and tenacity. If they give up the relationship, it'll be her choice, not Bruce's. She'll make the first step to break up or end it.

> *this is another relationship that won't last the test of time... love won't be enough to keep them together.*
>
> GEORGE ROMAN

When I was hired by Demi Moore to do Bruce Willis' birthday party, there were several stars there but not many brave enough to come and get a reading.

Pamela Anderson and Tommy Lee:

Now let's look at Pamela Anderson and Tommy Lee. They have 39 per cent in physical compatibility. Now, of course, Pamela Anderson is an attractive girl, but it's not the reason that Tommy Lee went after her. What we have here is a strong emotional compatibility of 71 per cent. This is very high. 71 per cent is not that far away from 100 per cent. So what we have is a couple that are together because they love each other, it's not for physical reasons. But they have a very low intellectual compatibility. They both have a tough time talking to each other and communicating with each other.

Once again, this is another relationship that won't last the test of time because without good communication and long term sexual compatibility, love won't be enough to keep them together.

As far as their faces are concerned, Tommy Lee is much more methodical. He's got the bony ridge where the eyebrows are, he's very methodical, he likes things set in a certain way. He's got these deep set eyes, he's a serious thinker. However, her eyes are also quite deep set. So they both tend to take things seriously.

He's got the nose for value and he's also possessive, you can tell by his ears. So he likes to collect things that are worth money and he'll only do things that are worth his time, energy or effort. He's a faithful person who's very direct in his speech, who's tenacious, who really pursues things, you can see from the jutting-out chin. With the skin, she's more in the middle, her skin's not really sensitive and thin, but it's not very thick either, so she'll let some things, comments, bounce off her and other things she'll take personally. He's got thicker skin, so he can let a lot more things bounce off him without taking them personally. So maybe when they argue in

their relationship - and they both have argumentative-
ness in their chins - it's likely that she'll take any comments
a little more personally than he does.

As far as the relationship's concerned, he'll stay in it as
long as he wants to and then, when he feels it's served its
purpose, which is how he judges things, he'll drop her.

> *Pamela Anderson is an attractive girl, but
> it's not the reason that Tommy Lee went
> after her. What we have here is a strong
> emotional compatibility of 71 per cent.*
> GEORGE ROMAN

Goldie Hawn and Kurt Russell:
Another interesting couple is Goldie Hawn and Kurt
Russell. We've got physical compatibility of 13 per cent,
so once again this is not the reason for them coming
together, the attraction was not physical. Their emotional reading's 29 per cent, which is very low, so there's
not a strong love bond there.

With these compatibilities, I think 60 per cent or
higher is needed. Now, overall, there is only a seven per
cent chance of getting 60 per cent in all three areas, but
you don't want it to be low in two out of the three and even
if it's low, you don't want it to be that low. Intellectually
they have a very high compatibility, 70 per cent. They can
talk to each other, they can communicate with each other,
they can almost read each other's minds because their
numbers are very close together, but with that low 13 per
cent which affects their sex drive and attractiveness to one
another and that low emotional 29 per cent, I think, once
age starts setting in for Goldie, she'll lose her attraction for
him and once that happens, their emotional bond would
not be strong enough to hold them together.

As far as face reading is concerned, Kurt Russell has a
high mental ceiling and a high forehead indicating that

once age starts setting in for Goldie, she'll lose her attraction for him...

he needs a lot of data, a lot of information. He also has this broad jaw line so we know he likes to be in charge, he likes to be in control. And Goldie Hawn has that too. As far as emotional expression goes, Goldie has wide eyes, which is very emotionally expressive - she almost wears her emotions on her sleeve. Kurt, on the other hand, has very little visibility in his eyes so he won't be as expressive emotionally. Now, of course, he's in the movie business, so he's paid to express his emotions. He has the nose for value so he doesn't do things unless they're worth his time, effort or money and he's also got a strong tendency towards possessiveness with the ears which means he'll do what he needs to do to get what he wants.

ROMANCE

> *love, like any other great thing, is a skill, not an object.*
>
> BARBARA DE ANGELIS

JULIE, SEX SYMBOL DYNASTY GROUP:
I am a believer in true love. I actually got my soul mate - tall, dark, rich, handsome - the whole package. He stood in line and joined my fan club in a comic book store and got a Polaroid photo of himself with me. Then he went home, packed his bags and came back to California.

We moved in together on the first date and I got a wedding dress two weeks later. We have been separated maybe twice in a year and a half. Once to go to a grocery store and once to go to a meeting and that's it. He packs my lunch, he goes on the sets with me, he does everything for me. His name is Kevin Eastman and he created the *Teenage Mutant Ninja Turtles*. And so we are going to have turtles instead of kids!

BARBARA DE ANGELIS:
'Making love work' is a phrase I use in all my infomercials and my shows. What it really means is understanding that love, like any other great thing, is a skill, not an object. And like all skill you need to practise it, you need to learn how to do it well, you need to get better at it. It's not going to just get better sitting on the shelf by itself. And that means you need to put time into a relationship, time into communicating, and realize that it's 100 per cent on one side and 100 per cent on the other, not even 50-50.

STEPHANIE BEACHAM:
Hollywood's most romantic couple? Seriously, there are some wonderful older couples, like Charlton and Lydia Heston, people that have been through all of it and have ended up 60 years later saying, 'My goodness, I like you.'

ELIZABETH KUSTER, AUTHOR OF *EXORCIZING YOUR EX:*
I love my parents, but I was brought up with that whole

thing that there is one man for you out there, your perfect man, and you will find him. And about two years ago, I realized that that is just a big lie. Who's to say there is just one guy out there? And if there is, what if he is, like, in Zimbabwe, and I never meet him, you know what I mean?

> *I am a believer in true love. I actually got my soul mate – tall, dark, rich, handsome – the whole package.*
>
> JULIE

I used to go out all the time out of fear that if he'd be out tonight and I thought that if I stayed home I wouldn't meet him! You know, it's crazy the things we put on ourselves. And then I had this huge realization that, you know what? I'm probably compatible with at least 20 guys, it's just that the timing is off, or maybe it's not right for me right now, or whatever, so I kind of stopped pushing it.

KELLY LANGE:
Well, take my last husband for instance. We were on our way to go skiing one Christmas and we stopped over in New York, at his apartment there, as a way to break up the trip. And he steered me down Fifth Avenue the next morning, and it was snowing, and he stopped in front of Tiffany, knelt down in the snow and proposed to me. Then we went into Tiffany and he had the ring ready. Romantic? Yes!

RUTH WEBB AND SHERRI SPILLANE, SCANDAL AGENTS:
Ruth: I have been seeing this attorney, he's a wonderful guy, he really is, but my God, he's cheap! I mean, I paid $67 for a bottle of champagne, as well as cooking dinner and going down to whatever that sex shop is and getting black lace underwear. And then I had to get on top of

him and then he went to sleep and I didn't even have an orgasm. I didn't have anything. And then he woke me up at 4:30 in the morning to go back to his office.

Sherri: I think you need a new date, Ruth.

EVELYN BROWN, AUTHOR:

I've found a way to keep romance alive. I produce personalized romance novels for couples at every stage in their romance, whether they're just starting out of have been married for 50 years. It gives them a whole new way of looking at their romance. My books are hardbound, one hundred page novels featuring you and your sweetheart as the hero and heroine. And I can write them about any couple.

I've written five novels altogether. They all have different plots, and are set in different locations and periods: Victorian England, California, Hawaii. I thought Hawaii was a very romantic place.

My newest one is called Calico Hearts, and it's set in the American West. She is a school teacher, he is the local sheriff and she doesn't like his job because it is so violent

> 66 *he stopped in front of Tiffany,*
> *knelt down in the snow*
> *and proposed to me.* 99
> KELLY LANGE

and so they have to work that out. Meanwhile there's a bad guy whose kind of stalking her and terrorizing the town and the sheriff's trying to prevent this and save her.

When I started out I thought that my clients would be women, because those are the ones who read romance novels. But it turns out it is the men that buy them as gifts for their wives or their sweethearts. They are bought by every age group, every income level, and I sell a lot on Valentine's Day, that's my big time, and Christmas of course.

DAVID KULMAN:

Men are very romantic. They send each other flowers, they walk on the beach hand in hand. They do everything like a Hallmark greeting card. I mean, gay people are exactly like straight people in every way except for their sex life.

DOE GENTRY:

I have a long-distance relationship. And he lives in East Lansing and he's thirteen years younger than me. I call him the baby boy.

CELIBACY & TEEN DATING

PHYLLIS DILLER:

I think it's a great thing to wait for the right person and marriage. I had one friend, Brooke Shields, who did that. She was a very celibate girl for many years, even though she's a great beauty. Now, of course, she crazy in love with Agassi, although they're not married yet.

BARBARA DE ANGELIS:

I think for certain periods in one's life, celibacy is an excellent idea. I spent several years deliberately celibate and it was wonderful. It made me question my values. It made me much more discriminating about who I spent any time with. I mean, if I wasn't going to have sex with him, did I even want to talk to him? And if I enjoyed talking to him, that was a good thing on its own and it's actually helped me realize that friendship is an essential part of a relationship. So I think more people should spend some time celibate.

My personal view is that being completely celibate, and not sleeping with your partner until marriage isn't a good idea. The reason I say that is that you find out a lot

" Those hormones click in and, man, nothing's going to stand in the way.

LOU PAGET

about somebody when you have sex with them. You find out things you'll never find out any other way. I've heard some real nightmare stories from women who dated Mr Wonderful and he was so sweet and they went to movies and they went out to dinner and everything was great and they got married and they got in bed and he said, 'By the way, here are some handcuffs that I'd like you to try on.'

Hidden personalities often come out in bed and I think it might be good to discover those before you actually say 'I do'.

STACY, TEENAGER:

True Love Waits is a commitment that teenagers and anybody can make. You make the commitment to God, yourself, your family, your future mate and future children that you will stay sexually pure until you get married. There's no age limit and you sign a little card that says you've made the promise. In some churches they even have a ring.

> *Hidden personalities often come out in bed and I think it might be good to discover those before you actually say 'I do'.*
>
> BARBARA DE ANGELIS

FRANCIS, TEENAGER:

My family is very supportive of my commitment to stay sexually pure until marriage. They think that it's great. With my close friends, they've either done it themselves or they are cool with it. When I meet people and they ask me about this commitment, I say it's cool and I think that everyone should do it. So they respect it.

TRUE LOVE PASTOR:

It's true that a lot of people say you should live together and be engaged to each other before you get married to

> *You make the commitment to God, yourself, your family,... that you will stay sexually pure until you get married.*
>
> STACY

test it out, to see if it will work and, in fact, when I was dating as a high school student the mother of one of my girlfriends suggested that I and her daughter do that.

But statistics have shown that couples who live together are more likely to get a divorce and more likely to be physically abused by their spouse. I think that in teens' lives now there is a mistrust. Because they think that if their boyfriend of girlfriend is going to shack up with them and have sex with them, will they do that with somebody else too? So it doesn't create the trust and commitment that a marriage has.

ALEXANDRA PAUL:

I haven't spoken to anyone in organizations like True Love Waits and the Pride of Virgins, but I've read articles about them, where the teenagers are encouraged to put off sex until marriage, and I think that the idea is really good. It puts an emphasis on other things besides sex at a time when your hormones are just everything, and everything is about sex.

LOU PAGET, CREATOR OF SEXUALITY SEMINARS:

The messages teenagers are constantly given about sex and sexuality is 'Don't!' and 'No!' So here they are growing up and they're being told 'No!' constantly. And then somehow they're supposed to go into a physical, intimate relationship with their partner but with what information?

All of us are born of sexuality and all of us have to learn about it. Now if someone's telling you that you have to do this or can't do that, that's their choice, not yours. I don't think that they're thinking when they do that.

Mother Nature created the most powerful drive going when she created the sex drive. I have been asked by

Mormon women to put together seminars for their daughters on oral and manual sex because they know their children need to know. Those hormones click in and, man, nothing's going to stand in the way. And they want their daughters to at least have the correct information. With information you have power and with power you have the ability to declare boundaries and that's what keeps you safe. Even though their daughters weren't going to be having intercourse their mothers still wanted them to have all the information.

OLIVIA GOLDSMITH:

So, they're 12 years old and they're dating? I don't think that's a problem. I think it's a problem that all female 12 year olds are on diets. That's a problem.

SUSAN POWTER:

Dating too young? Oh man, go to Tennessee, Kentucky. I mean, we are talking 12 and they date their cousins. A lot of inbreeding goes on there. Talk about dating too young! But then what's too young? I suppose it depends on your experience. I know that from my own experience that, unfortunately, I was never taught respect and love for my body and my being and my soul so I gave it away. You know it was like, 'Hey, you want to have sex?' I think it all depends on where you come from and how you are raised, on your family and what you are taught. I think that has an effect on the value that you place on yourself.

STEPHANIE BEACHAM:

This making out business, it starts about 11, doesn't it? I don't think they go all the way. I think they're quite good. I got very worried about what making out was. They ask me, 'Did you make out?' and that just means that you hold hands and, you know, have a lips-closed kiss. Do they start interacting between the sexes too young? No, I don't think so. There's a lot of just hanging out and being buddies. It's reasonably healthy.

The messages teenagers are constantly given about sex and sexuality is 'Don't!' and 'No!'

LOU PAGET

CHAPTER TWO

Mating in Hollywood

"
God created us in the form of man and woman to make love.

AMANDA DE CADANET,
TV PRESENTER AND ACTRESS

"

INTRODUCTION

Sex is a complicated business at the best of times, but factor in the added pressures of living in Hollywood and you are dealing with a maelstrom of insecurity. How on earth do you decide what to be and where to get it when there is so much to choose from?

On the one hand, there are the therapists and counsellors who battle against the rising tide of neuroses that constantly threaten to engulf their clients, while on the other, there is so much to choose from and many individuals in LA who are more than happy to indulge their fantasies and make it easier for others to indulge theirs.

If by day you work as a security guard, but by night you fancy dressing up in a body stocking and not much else, with a wooden spoon and a turkey baster tucked into your belt, that's fine. Sex parties abound for swingers in LA. Neither age, nor sexual proclivity are a problem behind closed doors, so long as you abide by club rules: practise safe sex, ask before you touch.

There are chokers and bug squishers, there are people who can't and those who can and can't stop. Phone sex, Internet sex, tantric sex and downright dirty sex. John keeps his erection drug in an old cigar tube in the freezer, 'Once you start kissing and getting sexual, boom! It just comes on real strong.'

Lou Paget will teach you how to give a blow job with a plastic penis on a plate. Naomi will attach a sex charm, made from stallion hair and other secret ingredients, to you pubic hair to ensure desirability at 50 paces.

Everyone has something to say about Hugh Grant's big night out on Sunset. Divine Brown says that she definitely helped his career along, Olivia Goldsmith says that, 'Any woman who can make a full, profitable and healthy career out of a single blow job, gets my respect', and Diane Conway, the Fairy Godmother says he was a bad, bad boy!

What they're interested in is the attention, the power, the intensity that they can arouse if they can get someone interested in them.

DR ROBERT WEISS

Fancy joining the Mile High Club? For $395, including champagne and clean sheets, Mile High Ventures will take you up for an hour and a half. And if the groans get too loud, they just turn up the CD player in the cockpit.

MILE HIGH CLUB

NICK, OWNER, MILE HIGH VENTURES:
The Mile High Club was started many years ago in the early '20s by the guy who invented the autopilot. He was the first person to have sex in an airplane at 5,500 feet - a mile above the earth.

I started Mile High Ventures as a way of building flight hours so I could get to work on the airlines. We outfitted this twin-engine plane with a whole feather bed in the back. We serve champagne and chocolate-covered strawberries and we have CD player on board and we take couples up to 5,500 feet and they have a great time.

Our services go beyond just the one-hour fight. We offer three course dinners on the airplane, a limousine to and from their home, premium champagne, longer flights, pretty much whatever they want.

I would say that the people who want to join are just your average couple who've been together for quite some time and they're looking for something unique and different to do. They've done the dinner thing and the movie and the romance and they're just looking for a more unusual experience to surprise one another with and this is right up their alley.

Unusual requests? Well, we've had some people show up with whipped cream and, you know, a bag full of all kinds of paraphernalia. I don't get to see what's in the bag, I have to fly the plane. But, I'm sure they bring all kinds of stuff.

...they're just looking for a more unusual experience to surprise one another...

NICK

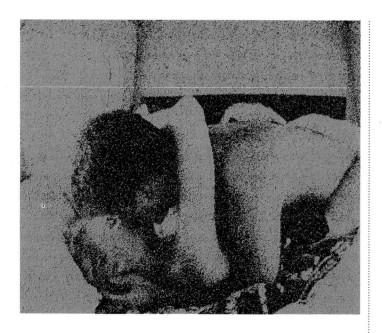

People who book the flight are mostly women. I'd say 95 per cent are women trying to romance their husbands and boyfriends.

The cost is $395 for the one-hour flight and that includes everything. We usually fly with two pilots for safety reasons.

> *Unusual requests? Well, we've had some people show up with whipped cream and, you know, a bag full of all kinds of paraphernalia.*
>
> NICK

Occasionally, we'll get the odd couple that will ask for some extra time while we're in-flight and they'll open up the partition and they'll tap us on the shoulder - and it gives us a bit of a fright because we're not used to being tapped on the shoulder in-flight - and they'll say, 'Can we stay up for another half an hour?' And we're like, 'Sure.' They pass through the credit card and away we go.

I would say about 95 to 100 per cent of our couples actually have sex on the airplane. I mean, they're going up there to join the Mile High Club. They have this huge interest in it. I think there's a fantasy out there in everybody to join the Mile High Club, either on an airliner or on a private plane. And, this is much more private and secure and they feel comfortable just to kind of let loose, get naked and have a good time.

Can we hear the couples? Not really. I mean, it's a pretty solid partition. You've got the engine noise and the music going, but I should say that on occasion we've heard a few howls coming from the back and, you know, we just have a chuckle.

Of course we change the sheets! We have probably about nine or ten sets of linen and they go straight to the cleaners and they're pressed and fresh when they get on the plane. It's like checking into the Four Seasons Hotel.

> *Of course we change the sheets! It's like checking into the Four Seasons Hotel.*
>
> NICK

GREG AND ALICE, MEMBERS, MILE HIGH CLUB:
Greg: It was great. It was really nice in a lot of ways. It was fun in terms of the height, the 5,500 feet, a mile high above the earth and and getting to see the whole city and then of course...
Alice: It was fun because it was private and sort of romantic and cosy. Very comfortable.

BURT WARD, ACTOR, BATMAN AND ROBIN:
I met this very beautiful French young lady and she was in economy and I was in first class. The plane was not too full as I remember and I invited her to come sit next to me. And I checked it out with the flight attendants and they said, 'Oh that's okay'. So one thing led to another and I said 'Hey listen, would you like to make love in the airplane? Would you like to join me in the Mile High Club?' And she say, 'Ooooh la la'.

So we decided we were going to try to make love in the lavatory. The opportunity finally came and she went in first and then I went in afterwards and it was really tight.

I mean it was really tight. Those lavatories, they don't have a lot of room. And we were starting to have a really good time and all of a sudden we hear, 'Return to your seat, turbulence'.

Well, let me tell you, if you ever try to make love in the middle of tremendous turbulence, it's up and down, left and right, and this way and that way, I mean it was like a Masters and Johnson moment. It was wild. And this girl kept getting noisier and noisier and I said, 'Shhh, we've gotta be a little quieter.' But she didn't hear me or couldn't care less and she finally climaxed and did this tremendous scream. Oh, my God, you know what I mean? And I was just, I was so embarrassed. I was afraid to come out of that bathroom. So we washed up in the sink. I mean it's like being two sardines in a can. It's like very tight in there. And she went back to her seat and I came out later and this flight attendant obviously knew what had gone on. And they wouldn't speak to me, they were so angry.

SEX ADDICTION

DAVE KULMAN, GAY MATCHMAKER:
It's a judgemental thing. Who's to say who's oversexed? If you have a partner who's the same as you, fine. But if you have a partner who's undersexed and you're oversexed, it's not going to work, is it? Unless you consider seeing someone else.

GEORGE FALARDEAU, PLAYBOY:
Oh, yes, I was addicted to sex. Can people be addicted to sex? Absolutely! Without a doubt. In some previous relationships and also in some recent ones, I was addicted to sex - I speak only for myself when I say that. I couldn't get enough sex during the day. My peak time was when

I was 19, 20, 21. Early on in my life I got divorced and I utilized those peak times to the best of my ability. I went through many, many women. I would have sex with a woman at lunch and then a dinner date with another woman and then I would go see someone else and have a nightcap. And my ego was strong and I felt good about it. I got a great thrill out of women being jealous over me, and arguing over me. And I found that I did become, and have become, literally addicted to sex. It went beyond a need to express my sexuality or for intimacy. It was anything, quick oral sex or whatever I could persuade the women to do.

I'm now in my mid-'40s I find that my interest and libido is still the same. Perhaps my endurance and my longevity isn't quite as it was, but I believe that it is. My interest and curiosity in sex and my on-going desire for it hasn't changed.

Many people in America are focused on sex and sex only. And I love sex. As soon as we get off camera I'll be thinking about it, I am thinking about it now. I think men think about sex every nanosecond.

I think men think about sex every nanosecond.

GEORGE FALARDEAU

ALANA STEWART, EX-WIFE OF
GEORGE HAMILTON AND ROD STEWART
There's addictions to everything now. You know, they have groups for any kind of addiction you can think of so I'm sure people could be addicted to sex, or maybe it's just an excuse to go out and be promiscuous. Who knows?

DOYLE BARNETT, COUPLES MEDIATOR:
Oh, I've had clients that are addicted to sex. But I think it's something that can be worked on. The whole problem with sex is that there's something going on underneath, some need.

Addicts could probably do a 12-step program like Alcoholics Anonymous. They have them for sex. Just as alcoholism is a compulsive disorder so is sex addiction. The clients I had, they had to have sex in every way

I know one particular movie star who's extremely famous and a big sex symbol. And yet he will jump on anything that breathes and he doesn't care what it looks like either.

JACKIE COLLINS,
AUTHOR

whatsoever. We had to try and find out what the need was that was going on underneath, what was it actually doing for them? What were they getting out of it? Then we were often able to replace that need with something else, something much healthier.

What makes them addicted? They've just picked out that particular thing to be compulsive about. I think it could just as easily have been food. It could have been exercise. It could have been money. It could have been anything. Sex just happens to be the one thing that they've chosen to be obsessed about.

DR PAT ALLEN, RELATIONSHIP THERAPIST:
Addiction is a chemical process. For some men it's the adrenalin of conquest, and the basis of that is violence. It's 'How many women can I get under my control?'

> *sometimes on the weekend it would be maybe one in the afternoon and one in the evening. It really isn't very hard when you schedule your time like that.*
>
> MARY ANNE

With women, we have this funny chemical called oxytocin that's released when we get turned on, and we tend to want more and more fixes. And when the oxytocin supply gets depleted, we go into a detox situation. So there are two kinds of sex junkies: adrenalin junkies, who use sexual stimulation to get their adrenalin going and oxytocin junkies who really like the feel of that chemical rush.

CARLA SINCLAIR, AUTHOR OF *NET CHICK*:
I think it's possible to become addicted to sex on the Internet because it's a very seductive place to be. And it's more fun to have sex with somebody on line than to do it by yourself.

MARY ANNE, SEX ADDICT:
Joe would call and I would say, 'I'll see you Monday'. And Dave would call and I'd say, 'Come by on Tuesday'. And sometimes on the weekend it would be maybe one in the afternoon and one in the evening. It really isn't very hard when you schedule your time like that. The only problem was I was finding that some of them wanted to see me more than just once. You know, they actually wanted to spend time with me on a more regular basis and I couldn't do that.

It was very exhilarating, very exciting, very thrilling,

right before and leading up to the act itself. But once that was over, the following day, I would find myself feeling kind of numb and empty inside and more depressed and I would almost wish I hadn't done it. I would feel a lot of remorse and some shame and guilt. I was being eaten up by those feelings of unworthiness. I felt very dirty inside.

> *That was the addiction for me: getting him to notice me, getting him to pay attention to me.*
> MARY ANNE

For me, the addiction was to the feelings I had when I met somebody new, getting his attention, getting him to respond. When I think about it, something would come over me and I would get this incredible, exhilarating feeling of somebody reacting to me and focusing totally on me. That was the addiction for me: getting him to notice me, getting him to pay attention to me. That was the obsession. Because once I got him and once we had sex, the sex did not do it for me, it was all those feelings prior to the sex. Afterward it would be, 'Okay, where's the next one?'

I would get this feeling of power and control and just walking into a grocery store I just knew all the men were looking at me, I just knew it, but I wasn't looking at anybody. It was just that feeling that all eyes were on me and I was the focus of everybody's attention and it gave me a feeling of such power. I loved it.

DR ROBERT WEISS, SEXUAL ADDICTION CONSULTANT: When I talk to someone who's sexually or romantically addicted they really don't talk about the goal of their behaviour being the sex. What they're interested in is the attention, the power, the intensity that they can arouse if they can get someone interested in them. I often hear sex addicts or sexual compulsives talk about the hunt, the chase, the thrill of the excitement, it's: when I can get him to look at me, when I can get her to pay attention to me, when we're cruising, when we see each other across a crowded room and our eyes meet.

I often say to recovering patients, 'You know that enchanted evening thing when you see a person across a crowded room and you know it's them and your eyes lock and there's no one else in the room and you're completely and utterly engaged with each other? Well when that happens, run in the other direction fast! Because that's the person with whom you'll probably play out the most problems.'

For example, I had a man come in recently, who's a pretty wealthy and successful financial manager here in Los Angeles, and he goes to bed with his wife around 11 at night and once he's sure she's asleep, about 12.30, he gets up and gets on the computer and he starts downloading pornography and getting into sexualized conversations with women and he'll be up until four or five in the morning several nights a week and then go back to bed at five and get up at seven and start his day.

Well, you can imagine what that does to his life, what that does to his sexual life with his wife, what that does to the energy and creativity he has in his work. He's tired, he's depressed, he has a secret life, he feels ashamed and he can't tell anyone.

Romantic and sexual addictions are all about secrets. Recovery and treatment are all about telling the truth, being accountable, taking responsibility.

It's not that these people are incredibly self-indulgent, it's that they don't know how to relax, they don't know how to give to themselves, they don't know how to create a peaceful moment for themselves.

People who come here, who are acting out with compulsive masturbation or pornography or the use of prostitutes, men who are going to the park and having sex or breaking their relationships up or having unsafe sex, they're not doing these things, in my experience,

Romantic and sexual addictions are all about secrets.

DR ROBERT WEISS

69

because they're bad people, they're not getting involved in intensive, destructive relationships because they want to hurt their wives. Their wives or partners may get harmed or feel angry and betrayed and hurt as a result and probably have every right to be, but these people are doing these kinds of things because that's how they cope, that's what they use to settle the chaos and confusion inside them.

Why would anyone with so much to risk, like Hugh Grant or Michael Douglas, someone who is handsome, successful, attractive and interesting, seek out situations that are going to cause them harm? I can't speak about those particular examples and say this person is an addict or that person isn't, but I can look at their behaviour and it tells me an awful lot about where they're coming from.

If someone engages in a sexual situation that they know has the potential to cause them or others tremendous harm, and yet they continue to engage in it, they're probably looking for a higher high. That to me says they have a problem, not that they're stupid or that they're joking around.

You know, the patients that I work with that have partners are really interesting. Married to a man, married to a woman, gay, straight, whatever, the betrayal that their partners talk about isn't that their partner went outside for sexual liaisons or even that they may have gone outside for romantic liaisons. It's that they've had this spouse who struggled with this sexual disorder for years and never told them. The betrayal that their partners are really wounded by is the secrecy. They're thinking, 'How could you do this stuff for all these years and not tell me? How could you shut me out of your life so completely for so many years?'

SAMANTHA, GUEST AT SEX PARTY:
I don't really believe in sex addiction. I think of addiction as being to something very specific, like a physiological dependence on certain drugs for example, so I don't

> *...that's what they use to settle the chaos and confusion inside them.*
>
> DR ROBERT WEISS

believe sex is something you can be addicted to. I do think that there are some people who use sex in ways that are definitely unhealthy, you know, who try to avoid intimacy or their feelings or whatever.

> *I don't think sex addiction is a problem in Hollywood. I think it's addiction to power, addiction to attention that's a problem.*
> BARBARA DE ANGELIS

People use a lot of things like that. People use exercise, they use work, some people use falling in love and romance. But I'm very suspicious of the whole idea of sex addiction. I think it's something people use against you if they think you're having too much sex or the wrong kinds of sex. I've read a couple of books on sex addiction, and I can see the kinds of things they use to prove that somebody is a sex addict.

I mean, they use things like masturbating a lot, using pornography, practising sado-masochism, having multiple partners, being interested in sex for sex's sake and not as part of a relationship. I think all those things are fine, I don't have a problem with them. I do all of them myself and I don't feel it's unhealthy. I think that the whole idea of sex addiction is a way of repressing sexuality, a way of saying: you're crossing sexual boundaries that we don't want you to cross.

BARBARA DE ANGELIS,
MARRIAGE COUNSELLOR AND THERAPIST:
I don't think sex addiction is a problem in Hollywood. I think it's addiction to power, addiction to attention that's a problem.

I was working with a young actress last week, who was telling me that every time she sees a man, anywhere, she has to know he's paying attention to her, she has to know that he's noticed her, that he's attracted to her even if he's married or taken and she gets a tremendous thrill out of it. She knows it's a problem, but it's a need she has.

BURT WARD:
I don't know about sex addiction. I think availability is really the issue. If people have availability to that all the time, they're gonna take it because it's pleasurable. I don't think actors are any more sexually endowed or sexually interested in other people. But they have more opportunities and they take them up.

DENNIS FRANZ, ACTOR, *NYPD BLUE*:
People are coming here for fame and fortune and to make a lot of money and sometimes that creates sort of bizarre personalities in people.

KENNEDY, PRESENTER, MTV:
I've never been addicted to sex. I've certainly been addicted to chocolate though. God forbid that I should combine the two someday.

CELEBRITIES AND SEX

BURT WARD:
You have to understand, when I started in *Batman* I was a very naive kid. I was 20 years old. I was married at the time and the marriage didn't last too long because there was a lot of pressure and terrible long hours. But I remember I almost got fired because I was trying to be so honourable to my wife that I refused to kiss another actress on the cheek. With my first marriage, we were both very young, you know. And she became very jealous and would come to the set every day and there was such

tension that finally it was too much for me. I needed space and I called it quits. I met Adam West, who played Batman and immediately introduced me to the wildest sexual debauchery you could imagine. I met just about every kind of wild and crazy person. Within a few months my marriage had dissolved and Adam and I were like two hungry sharks in a world of unlimited halibut. Actually, I think Adam was more like a killer whale in the world of plankton.

I've had a lot of fun. I must tell you, Adam and I have really partied very heavily. I mean, we got involved with probably around ten thousand women in the course of 20 years of making personal appearances and signing autographs. Everywhere we went. It was the thing during the '60s. It's a different world now. You can't have that open sexuality that you had back in the '60s. That was the period of free love and flower children and girls chased guys as much as guys chased girls. And it was very open, you know.

...Adam and I were like two hungry sharks in a world of unlimited halibut.

BURT WARD

We were having this party... Adam was on one bed with his girl and I was on another bed with my girl, so, I guess that's double dating.

BURT WARD

Adam and I never exactly double dated. But, we did have some rather wild experiences. There was one time in a Holiday Inn in upstate New York where we'd done a car show and signed autographs. Afterwards, we went upstairs and we actually had a couple of girls in his room that we were going to party with and then, waiting for us across the hall in my room, were two more girls.

So, we were having this party with these girls and, I'm telling you, Adam was on one bed with his girl and I was on another bed with my girl, so, I guess that's double dating and we were going at it, really having a wild time.

And afterwards, I reminded Adam: 'You know, we've got these other ladies waiting for us over there and it'd be really impolite not to go over and see them.' And Adam says to me, in that deep voice of his, 'Now look Burt, I'm a grown man, you know, but you're a kid. We've got to go across this hallway and neither of us have any clothes on. I want you to go across and open the door with your key. When the door is open, I'm gonna come out, close the door, run across the hallway, and we'll be with these two girls'. And I said, 'Holy age discrimination!'

So, anyway, I finally did it. And Adam comes rushing out, he pulls his door closed, he runs over to my door and I lock him in the hallway. And the reason I did that is because for all these years - and I probably should have stated this at the beginning - he used to upstage me. He'd stand right in front of me, he'd block me and whenever I'd say, 'Adam, why are you doing this to me? You're ruining my shot!,' he'd say, 'I'm sorry Burt, I had to do it.'

> *She was much bigger than I was. Huge muscles! She looked more like Batman than Batman did!*
>
> BURT WARD

Well, here we were, with him locked in the hallway and he says, 'Burt open this door. Open it now!' And I said, 'Sorry Adam. I had to do it.' And he said, 'What are you talking about? Open this door now!' But all I would say was, 'Sorry Adam. I had to do it.'

So, I got engrossed and forgot about him. It was an hour and a half later before I remembered that I had left him in the hallway. He had nowhere to go, so I went out in the hallway to look for him but he was gone.

Well, I looked down at the end of the hallway and there was a window open out on to the fire escape. And this is the dead of winter. So I walked down to the end

*I mean
they don't
call me the
Boy Wonder
for nothing.*

BURT WARD

and I heard this sneeze. And I looked out on this fire escape and there was this figure all crouched over and completely covered with snow. I looked a little closer and sure enough, it was a familiar face. I mean they don't call me the Boy Wonder for nothing.

There was one lady - a body builder - who I went out with and she was really something. I mean, it was one of the most embarrassing times of my life because she was much bigger than I was. Huge muscles! She looked more like Batman than Batman did! And we had this wild time at my beach house in Malibu and I made this very gallant statement about carrying her to bed. But when I actually went to lift her I couldn't. She was too heavy. So in the end she carried me to bed. It was extremely embarrassing.

Did Batman and Robin have an affair? No. Although some psychiatrists back in the '50s complained that they thought the comic represented a dream-wish of two homosexuals.

And while I was filming the series, people would ask me, 'Don't you think that Batman and Robin's relationship is strange and unnatural?" And I'd say 'Hey, wait a minute.

> *...he's been caught with his Bat trunks down.*
>
> BURT WARD

What's so strange and unnatural about two guys who run around wearing tights and live together? Big deal!'

Adam was sort of like a role model for me. For a young kid growing up, who better to be a role model than Batman? And this Batman really did have a secret identity. He would tell me things that were so strange and kinky - he was a very wild man.

I asked Adam West to be my best man at my wedding because I really liked Adam and although we were in competition, there were lots of times when we were really good friends and partied together, in some cases literally cheek to cheek, if you know what I'm saying.

I think Adam is basically hysterical about my book. I tell everybody that it's unfortunate but he's been caught with his Bat trunks down. Fortunately Adam was married, and still is to the same lady, while the stuff that I talk about in the book was happening. And it wasn't that I was trying to get him in trouble, but I couldn't leave him out of the book because we did a lot of these things together. It was part of the Batman and Robin partying scene. We had this special line between the two of us: whenever we one of us would have great sex, and the other one asked 'Well how was it?' We would always, 'Beyond decadence'.

So, of course, I couldn't leave him out of the story. But he can certainly deny that it happened. Maybe he can sell that. But I don't think so.

Adam has accused me of having made up the stuff in my book, all of which is true. But he sure has come up

> *I really liked Adam and although we were in competition, there were lots of times when we were really good friends and partied together, in some cases literally - cheek to cheek.*
>
> BURT WARD

with some very funny comments. During one interview he said, 'Burt's book is so full of bologna that he should open a delicatessen. But he'd probably be sued for food poisoning.' Well, that's a pretty cute line. That's pretty creative.

> *We had this special line between the two of us: whenever we one of us would have great sex, and the other one asked 'Well how was it?' We would say, 'Beyond decadence'.*
>
> BURT WARD

I don't know exactly how many lovers I've had. I never kept track of it. I mean, you'd really have to work at it to keep those kinds of numbers. I never considered it to be something of importance. Based on if I were to take any given weekend and then multiply that by the number of weeks that I was on the road and the number of years I did it... I'm sure thousands.

Anybody as promiscuous today as we were back then would really be taking chances with their life. I certainly wouldn't do that today.

People frequently ask me, 'How could you have that many wild and crazy experiences?' Well, when you're on the road for 25 to 30 years, doing 350 cities, a lot of stuff happens. There's a lot more that's not actually in the book.

Because Adam challenged me in the press about the truth of these stories in my book, I went on national television and made an announcement, 'Because Adam West has accused me of exaggerating and not telling the truth, I want all the ladies out there who during the last 30 years, had sex with either Adam West or myself, to write to my post office box, because I'm gonna come back on national television with a wheel-barrow full of letters to prove that everything that I said was true.'

Well, once Adam heard that I was getting thousands of letters from across the country of the affairs we'd both had, he quickly took back what he'd said and stopped doing interviews because that's the last thing he wanted - me on national television - while he and his wife watched me reading the letters.

There is an endless supply of women when you're famous, if that's what you want. It's not that these women think that they're giving themselves to you. It's that they think they want a part of you, so you're chased vigorously. And it makes some performers really back off and not want to get involved.

You know, I grew up in a conservative family. Then I was exposed to all this wild Hollywood craziness and it ruined my marriage. But I never cheated on my wife - I asked for a divorce before I started to do this stuff because I saw that it was affecting both my life and my career. And for 17 years I partied, you know, and finally met the girl of my dreams and settled down. I'm thrilled to be married.

Do actors have a higher sex drive than other people? No, I think actors have the same sex drive as everyone else. There are some actors that take themselves really seriously and they are least qualified to live up to their image. Either they're on drugs or they're on alcohol, or they're so busy admiring themselves that they have no time for the ladies. But women don't want insensitive men. They like sensitive, caring men. And if someone is a celebrity, and treats them with respect at the same time, they love that.

> *There is an endless supply of women when you're famous.*
>
> BURT WARD

> *You need to experience things. And for me it was more experience than I expected.*
>
> BURT WARD

CELEBRITIES AND PROSTITUTES

DR DAVID LEVY, PSYCHOLOGIST:
People desire sex and they have sex for many reasons. For some people it's an expression of intimacy and compassion. For others, sex is naughty and that's part of the excitement. Prostitution is naughty; so having sex with a prostitute might add to sexual excitement.

DIVINE BROWN, EX-PROSTITUTE:
How much you can make in an evening depends on how the night is, what time of the month it is. It's a round-season thing, you know. So, it varies. You can make good money if the weekend is good, if people have been paid during the week.

> *Hugh wanted me totally, all of me, from my toenails to my fingernails.*
>
> DIVINE BROWN

One day I'm just going to give a really huge bash for women, for all my old friends. You know, invite everybody 'cause I miss them, but I don't miss the cold nights.

It can get bad. It can get so bad that you'll never be seen again. A lot of girls that I knew never came back and then they were found dead, you know, beat in the head. It's rough out there.

The night I met Hugh Grant, I can't remember really, it was just a normal night, with a normal guy that needed some female company, wanted some attention. We call it attention in the US. And that's what the women are out there for, to give a guy a little bit of attention for a little bit of time. But, of course, time is money and money is time.

I'd never even heard of the guy. Not at all. When it hit the fan six hours later, after I got busted, they had my face all over the news and his face all over the news. I got busted at, like, one in that morning and I was on the six o'clock news that morning. And from then on, whenever they could fit it in, my name came up.

I was like, 'Oh, God what did this guy do to me? What did I do to this guy?' I was thinking, I used the condom but did he give me something? Was he exposed to something and exposed me and was a carrier? I was thinking all kinds of things. I was really scared.

> *I was tired. I didn't want to be out there and the jackpot came through.*
> DIVINE BROWN

Yeah, I think I helped his career. Very much so. Of course, I guess he was a well-known guy in some places 'cause during the time he was making that movie. But, you know, it was a coincidence that that same morning he had a big press interview. And he came out and did

> *Evidently, she [Liz Hurley] wasn't doing what momma does at home best.*
>
> DIVINE BROWN

something like that to boost the movie up or whatever. And it really did - a lot of people wanted to see this guy in action to see who he was. So that brought the people to the box office. And I think I really made his career successful. He's on his third movie now.

In Hollywood, everybody cruises. All the celebrities go out cruising, you know, just to have a good time, just to see who's out. There's nothing wrong with that, not at all.

I've met a couple of celebrities. All kinds. You get movie actors, you get music stars, you get the models, the basketball players, you know, you get a variety. Everybody that's doing something, they're out. You can see them cruising, you can see them in the store buying a hamburger or something, you know. But not everybody's out on Sunset trying to look for a date or a female that's walking with high heels on and looking good to them. They might pull over and say, 'Hey girl! What's going on?' and then leave. But Hollywood is a party town, you know.

Hugh - he was lonely. When you have a woman that's always working and doesn't have time or you're both working, you have to do something in between and that's what he did. But he didn't do it the right way.

My new movie's a porno. It's called the *Sunset and Divine British Experience*. Kim Kintain, another porn star, is in it. And it's a really good movie. I've seen other pornos but, this one, it seems different. Not because I'm in it, but because it's a unique video. It's better for some reason, like they put more effort in it than other porno movies. And it's a re-enactment of what happened that night with me and Hugh Grant.

My children? I have a boy and two daughters. They think I'm a TV news reporter, they see me on the news so much. But as they get older I intend to talk to them and really explain to them what happened and why I was on TV so much.

Hugh told me what he wanted but he didn't have enough for what he wanted so I told him what he was

> *Hugh - he was lonely. Every guy has a fantasy.*
>
> DIVINE BROWN

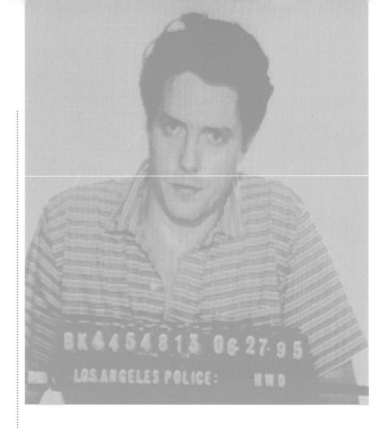

going to get. He wanted me totally, all of me, from my toenails to my fingernails. And I was like, 'No buddy, I'm sorry, let me see your wallet. Give me your wallet.' It was a funny night. It was hilarious though it was slow. I was tired, I didn't want to be out there and the jackpot came through. But it was like a common, normal night.

I miss just being out there, you know. Not that I'm bragging up on it. But, I miss my friends. When I needed someone to help me get one guy off me or another guy was trying to do something bad, you have friends that really look after you out there.

Evidently she [Liz Hurley] wasn't doing what momma does at home best, you know. He was lonely, wanted something different. Every guy has a fantasy.

DIANE CONWAY, COMDIENNE AND FAIRY GODMOTHER: Hugh Grant, what a nitwit he was. You know, he could have picked a more discreet way to do that in LA. Heidi Fleiss could have fixed him up with somebody and snuck him in the back door and probably got him a better quality thing. But that idiot probably got a heat on, had a few too many and went out on Sunset Boulevard. Any nitwit knows not to do that and of course he gets arrested. They're just waiting for people there. So he was bad. Bad, bad boy!

BRENDA LOVE, AUTHOR OF
ENCYCLOPEDIA OF UNUSUAL SEXUAL PRACTICES:
People use prostitutes for a lot of different reasons. One is anonymity which didn't work with Hugh Grant!

KELLY LANGE, AUTHOR OF
TROPHY WIVES AND BROADCASTER:
Maybe the danger was part of it. Certainly, he could afford a call girl. You can practically get them in the yellow pages here and have somebody discreetly come to your room, but he didn't choose to do it that way.

Ms Divine Brown has made a career out of this, as anybody who was smart and is an opportunist would. Good for her, more power to her. I don't hold it against her at all.

OLIVIA GOLDSMITH, AUTHOR OF *FIRST WIVES CLUB*:
I've talked to a fairly powerful Hollywood mogul about why a man like Hugh Grant, who can obviously have any woman he wants, and has one, apparently, who seems quite lovely, would want to go with a black hooker? And the answer is that - and this is not based on my own experiences, it's what my friend told me - when you can have anyone you want and there's intense pressure from women to take them, it's such a relief to just pay for it and have it done with.

I think any woman who can make a full career, a full, profitable career out of a single blow job, gets my respect. It's America. It's life in the fast lane. Well, actually, I think they were parked, but you know what I mean.

SHERRI SPILLANE, SCANDAL AGENT:
There must have been something missing in his life. Why

do men turn to hookers? If they're not getting what they want at home, if they have an incredible sex drive that can't be fulfilled, if they're just feeling a little tacky that night. I don't know what drove Hugh to Sunset Strip. I only know that he's probably the sorriest man alive that he ever made that trip.

Honestly, I think it did help his career. He was known but he's more known than ever, and I think the man should be thankful to God and everyone around him that Elizabeth Hurley took him back.

I wouldn't have, I wouldn't touch him with a ten-foot

> *It's like food. Sometimes you want a gourmet meal, sometimes you want a hamburger. I guess he was in the mood for a hot dog.*
>
> JACKIE COLLINS

pole, not after he's been where he's been. I mean shame on that boy! You can do better than Sunset Strip.

And he said he only had $30 on him. I find that hard to believe. Maybe he didn't want anybody to know who he was, maybe he figured a high-class hooker would know who he was, or maybe he really wanted to get down and dirty.

GENA LEE NOLIN:
Hugh is somebody that I've definitely looked up to as an actor. He's extremely talented.

ROGER CLINTON, BROTHER OF BILL:
Good people make mistakes, good people do dumb things. You know, I can attest to that.

BRIDGET, ESCORT:
I felt badly for Heidi. I don't know her personally but we had a mutual friend - who is now dead - so I know of her

> *Honestly, it did help his career... I think the man should be grateful to God and everyone that Elizabeth Hurley took him back.*
>
> SHERRI SPILLANE,
> SCANDAL AGENT

and I feel badly for her. She was trying to run a business and make some money and unfortunately I think she got involved with some sort of political situation and she paid the price for that.

I don't think that what she was doing was right. But I don't think that what she was doing was wrong either. Now she's trying to put her life back together. I hope that she doesn't go back to jail. I dont think that anyone should go to jail for what she has done.

I don't know the extent to which she may have committed a criminal act as far as income tax or anything else goes. But as far as her little ring of girls is concerned, I don't think that anyone was hurt. It makes me a little bit angry that she's taking the blame for so much publicity and the men that used her services are not.

I think that Madam Alex was probably more connected than Heidi was. She was older and more experienced. And I don't know if she got away with it. She was also dragged through the court system.

DOYLE BARNETT:

Prostitution? You know, it's interesting. Everyone's just so busy and sex and relationships are so complicated. Especially now that men are getting more involved with their emotions, more in tune with them. They can't just tell the woman what to do like they used to and keep it simple.

And I do think sex is a physical need for many people. I think that's not necessarily an unhealthy thing.

DENNIS LOWE, MARRIAGE THERAPIST:

When you're away from home, away from your normal contacts and from your family members, people find themselves in situations where they are vulnerable to making decisions and doing things that they wouldn't otherwise do. And this is certainly not to excuse Hugh Grant's behaviour but I think that these are exactly the kinds of things that happen all the time when people are away from home.

EMILY SCOTT-LOWE, MARRIAGE THERAPIST:
Some people like the excitement of taking a risk. And having any extramarital relationship fuels the excitement of taking a risk and getting away with it.

PHYLLIS DILLER, COMEDIENNE:
Hugh Grant was an unknown name until he got hooked up with the hooker, Divine Brown. What a name! She is brown and she is divine and no one would ever have heard of her if she hadn't got mixed up with a movie star. Is that bad? Let me think. Well you know, Andy Warhol, my dear friend, said that everyone will have 15 minutes of fame and he certainly hit the nail on the head.

It made Hugh Grant's name. I would not have known his name if I had not read all that garbage.

And I think it got her six figures. She was working for 60 bucks and then went to 300,000. It did her more good than it did anybody, I believe.

In my opinion, it's perpetuating a negative image of women.

AMANDA DE CADANET

BARBARA DE ANGELIS:
It was obvious to me and a lot of other experts in Los Angeles when the whole Hugh Grant incident happened, that he obviously didn't need to find a prostitute for sex. He has a beautiful woman in his life. And he wasn't completely intoxicated or coked out, so that he didn't know what he was doing. To me his unconscious was working very strongly. The little demon voice inside said to him, 'You're not good enough and you don't deserve it', and in a sense tried to sabotage his career - unsuccessfully. And that's really interesting.

SUSAN POWTER, FITNESS GURU:
Why did he do it? Beause he was horny and he wanted oral sex and Elizabeth wasn't there to give it to him.

I don't know. I don't think it was the brightest decision. I mean I think the guy is just cute as hell and bright and articulate and funny and my question to Hugh is, 'Man, why didn't you have her come to the hotel room?'

That's why I think there was some intoxication involved because have ten of them come to your hotel room, you can afford it, babe.

Nobody had to know, you know. Did he want to get caught?

No, I don't even think he was thinking that much. He just thought, 'Hey, oral sex. Let's go.' I think it was that basic, you know.

AMANDA DE CADANET:

There's a lot of prostitution in this town, going from street-side hooking to high-class call girls. It's an age-old profession. I feel for the women that do it because it's very sad, you know, being intimate with somebody, sharing your body with somebody you don't know, who you don't care about.

I don't care if anyone says it doesn't mean anything. You know in your soul it does. God created us in the form of man and woman to make love and be intimate with somebody for the sole purpose of procreating - which is not cool because every time you have sex you don't want to have a baby! - so it's kind of abusing yourself.

There's a lot of it, I see quite a lot. I was at this party the other night there were so many hookers. In my opinion, it's perpetuating a negative image of women. I was talking about this with somebody last night and I asked him, 'Why do you pay for sex?' And he answered, 'I pay them to leave.' So people who do that don't have to deal with intimacy and most people have intimacy issues. And if somebody goes to a prostitute, it's a very contained environment, it's very clear. You pay for this, you do this and then you go.

I have very mixed views. I feel for the women that do it. Some of them they do have a necessity because they have drug addictions or children to support or they have major problems and that's the only way they can earn enough money. On the other hand, it's just not doing womenkind any favours.

> *...it's very clear...you pay for this, you do this and then you go.*
>
> AMANDA DE CADANET

> *I totally believe in prostitution. I think they should legalize prostitution and leave everybody alone.*
>
> JOAN RIVERS

JACKIE COLLINS:

The thing with call girls in Hollywood is that they are always very beautiful and very classy because, think about it: they win a beauty contest in some little town, then they come out to Hollywood full of ambitions and dreams, they arrive here on the bus or the plane. They kind of go through that whole playboy mansion syndrome, where a lot of people sample their charms. Then they get a little disillusioned, they look around and say, 'Why am I giving it away for free?' Then one of the madams gets hold of them and the madam is usually a very beautiful woman in her 30s who has been through that whole scene, and she says to the girl, 'Hey, honey, you could be making thousands of dollars a night. Why are you giving it away? You're not going to be a movie star. Come and join me.'

JOAN RIVERS, COMEDIENNE:

I don't understand why they go to a madam. Someone like Charlie Sheen, who could have any girl he wants. I could understand a poor schmucky guy who doesn't know how to take a girl, who's not attractive.

I totally believe in prostitution. I think they should legalize prostitution and leave everybody alone.

Someone explained to me that in Hollywood some men are so busy and so driven that they haven't even got the time to court a woman, let alone take her out for dinner. They just want to, 'Get her up here for 20 minutes, then get rid of her, I've got to get to the studio.'

Hugh Grant, who was a second rate movie star, pulled his pants down in a car and became a giant star. And Divine Brown is a household name now. So that sends a great message to everyone, doesn't it?

Divine Brown was suddenly doing commercials, she was doing an ad in a magazine, she suddenly became one of those 15-minute celebrities Andy Warhol talked about. And good for her! This poor old hooker on the street, hopping into cars wearing knee pads. Not an easy life.

PORN AND RELATIONSHIPS

NIKI STIRLING, PORN STAR:
My husband completely supports my work [as a porn star]. We went into this industry together and he enjoys the fact that I can experiment with other men on screen, he enjoys watching me. He can come on set and watch me or he can watch me on video. He enjoys hearing about my scenes when I come home. It turns us both on. He's proud of what I do, he doesn't feel I'm being degraded.

I think at first my family was concerned that I was doing it for the wrong reasons. But once they understood that I'm actually a nymphomaniac and getting my sexual fixes in a safe environment and having a lot of fun and I'm not getting harmed or being taken advantage by anyone and I know what I'm doing, I've got a head on my shoulders, they accepted it. And they're supportive. Most of the time they want to see photos and hear about the latest movies I've been in.

ALEXANDRA PAUL, ACTRESS, *BAYWATCH*:
I think pornography within a relationship can be great. Even if only one person in the relationship gets turned on by pornography, that's still okay. I guess where it becomes dangerous is if the person who's into the pornography becomes obsessed with just the pornography.

NINA HARTLEY, PORN STAR:
It is unequivocally true that adult movies can help people's sex lives. First and foremost it really helps spice up a monogamous marriage and if you both value monogamy it is a wonderful tool to help keep that spark alive. Monogamy's difficult. Especially after you have children maybe you're not as beautiful as you once were and you're tired with the kids, the job, the moving and all the pressures.

> *It is true that adult movies can help people's sex lives.*
>
> NINA HARTLEY

And you finally get the kids to bed and you have 30 minutes. Well, you can spend 30 minutes trying to get in the mood or you can spend ten minutes watching a video to get in the mood and have good sex. I know that for me if the mood is right you can have mutually satisfying sex in 20 minutes. You can save the big stuff for the weekends. So pornography definitely is helpful for people who wish to preserve monogamy.

If my husband gets on the Internet and downloads a naked girl dancing for him, would I be upset? Yeah!

GENA LEE NOLIN, ACTRESS, *BAYWATCH*

Anything that promotes sexual contact between a couple is a positive thing and certainly for single people it's helpful as a masturbatory device. Many men find out what a clitoris is by looking at an adult video. Where is it? What can you do to it? And I know a lot of women who walk around thinking that they're misshapen or deformed because they've never seen anyone else. We're not taught to examine ourselves and we're not allowed to look at anybody else. So women can look at a video and realize that their vulvas are not weird.

PHONE SEX AND COMPUTER SEX

SHERI, PHONE SEX ACTRESS:
Phone sex is about fulfilling the callers' fantasies. There are married out in the Midwest and in their daily, average life, they don't hear women talk to them the way I talk to them. I tell them the things they need to hear to help them through their hectic, busy lives.

Usually they pay between $20 and $40. That's about average. I need to stay on the line with each client for at least eight minutes. But I don't sit down and time myself with each caller. For the guys that want to talk, I'll talk to them. And for the guys that don't want to talk, I'll just give them the sex they want.

It was very difficult at first. I didn't know what to say. I'd never even said the word 'pussy' before. To begin with my partner thought it was interesting, he encouraged me to do this. He thought it would make me more sexual and it did, without a doubt. But then he became a little jealous. Now he's kind of okay with it, he's learning how to cope with it.

I tell the callers that I'm 21 years old. If change my description around too much, they know, and they'll go, 'Oh, Lisa, didn't you have different measurements last time.' So I need to keep them the same. But I do have two different descriptions: a tall description for the tall men, and short, more realistic description for the guys I think that might call me back. For the guys that I know only call

...in their daily, average life, they don't hear women talk to them the way I talk to them.
SHERI

once in a while, I make myself into Barbie. I say I'm five foot eight my measurements are 39-24-34, and I have long, straight blonde hair down to my butt and big green eyes and a beautiful California tan, and I just go all out.

Well, they're usually at home in their bedroom, all alone. No, I don't think they're cheating at all. In fact, if they're married, they'll say where their wife is. They're pretty honest. They'll say they're married or that they have a girlfriend. And often sex is good, but it's not what they want. Men want to hear a woman talk to them while they're having sex. With most men - and I don't mean every guy, just the ones who call me - I pretty much know what they want want.

CHERIE, PHONE SEX ACTRESS:
What is phone sex? Well, it's every man's and every woman's fantasy. Whatever they want, you act it out. It can be anything you could possibly imagine.

I've been doing it now for about four months and I really like it. It's quite a challenge because I used to be a very shy person and this was a way of kind of drawing me out of my shell. So, it's been a real experience.

I don't know if I'd want to choose it as a career, but it's something fun to do. My husband thinks it's a kick. I wasn't sure at first when I told him that I got a job doing phone sex. He looked at me a little strangely but he's fine with it now. He doesn't have a problem. He's never heard me on the line, though. He just takes guesses at what I'm saying.

Yeah, I do get bored a lot when I'm on-line. But I try to keep busy, I do needlepoint or crossword puzzles or some stuff on some costumes.

There are usually two busy times. First thing in the morning, when guys are just getting up and they want to feel good before they go to work, and then it picks up again in the evening, usually about seven thirty, eight o'clock because guys are coming home from work or, if they're calling from back East they just want it before

Yeah, I do get bored a lot when I'm on-line. But I try to keep busy...

CHERIE

they go to bed, to make themselves feel good before they hit the sack.

I had a guy calling from his job and I could only assume he was in an office somewhere. I was ready to bring him to his peak and somebody walked in on him. All I heard in the background was, 'What the hell are you doing?' and then over the line, 'Oh, shit!' and the guy hung up.

You know, it happens. I'm amazed that people call from work, they call from their girlfriend's houses and from their cars. I had one guy who was on the freeway and he called from his car phone and I didn't even want to know.

> *Maybe if my lover called me it would be wonderful. But, no, not a stranger.*
> ROBERT BLOOM

ROBERT BLOOM, LONELY HEART:
Phone sex is not for me. That doesn't turn me on or do anything for me in any way. No, I find it a little on the trashy side. So I don't get a kick out of phone sex, no. I've never tried it. Maybe if my lover called me it would be wonderful. But, no, not a stranger.

CARLA SINCLAIR:
I think with these video phone sex deals, you type in sentences to the person on the other end and it's live. And they in return will interact with you and if they like you, they can do things for you. Take off their clothes or, you know, have sex with themselves. And I think the typing can get pretty difficult at times for the person getting the show.

BARBARA DE ANGELIS:
I don't think sex with anyone but your partner is a good idea. Whether it's on the phone, whether it's in a car,

whether it's in a hotel. I think you get the same group of people with unhappy marriages, who don't feel satisfied with their partners and don't know what to do about it, and rather than go out and have an affair, which they might have done in the '80s, now there's AIDS, people are petrified. So, they get on their computer and they have on-line sex or they have phone sex.

The problem is age-old, the technique may be new, but it's really the same issue. You're not happy in your relationship and rather than fixing it, you're covering it up and going somewhere else. And it's a very temporary solution and one that's really going to do a lot more damage than good.

> *You're not happy in your relationship and rather than fixing it, you're covering it up and going somewhere else.*
>
> BARBARA DE ANGELIS

I think infidelity, whether you physically do it, whether you talk about it, whether you describe it, or whether you think about it incessantly, is still infidelity. Just because your body is not participating in something, doesn't mean you're not participating, in fact you could probably have a much stronger experience in fantasy than you do physically because reality could turn out to be terrible but in your fantasy world everything's perfect. So when I hear from wives, 'My husband says all he did is call someone up and he says that doesn't count as cheating' I tell them it absolutely does.

If you're in a relationship with someone's who's addicted to sex, addicted to pornography, is on-line having affairs, you have a serious marital problem. You need instant counselling, you need a major confrontation, and his saying 'I won't do it anymore' isn't enough, why he's doing it is the real issue. Any affair is just a symptom of a deeper problem.

BACHELOR AUCTIONS

GEORGE FALARDEAU:
There are several bachelor auctions in American and the one in LA is one of the bigger ones. It's an opportunity for women to go to and bid for single males. And the money usually goes to a charitable cause. It also allows women to be in a place uncontrolled by men where they can openly say and do what they want to do. At this one bachelor auction in LA there were thousands of women and only 40 men. And the women had a good time and felt empowered.

> *...the women had a good time and felt empowered.*
>
> GEORGE FALARDEAU

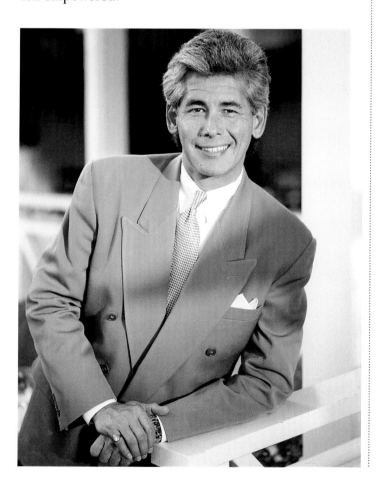

> *It was a bidding frenzy of women that were just beside themselves to get a date with George [Clooney]*

GEORGE FALARDEAU

What's it like to be a guy being auctioned at one of these events? Well, in the meeting beforehand, they pump you up and tell you what to say and how to act. And you are very, very nervous. Then you go into a room with 40 men and you look at your competition and at big stars, guys like George Clooney, and you feel intimidated. You think they're probably going to go for the biggest money and no one is going to bid for you. That was my biggest concern.

So then they fill you up with alcohol and feed you and check your tux and make sure you look right. And I was even more intimidated seeing all the men dressed up.

The first thing they have is this cocktail party, which lasts about an hour. And they send you out there with, 'Go for it and the women will love ya'. And of course I tried to be as charming as I possibly could be and it wasn't actually all that difficult. The women really were talkative and attractive and outgoing and easy to meet.

They tell you that when you go into the auction you are going to get given many business cards and they teach you to put the phone numbers of the women that you want to date in your right pocket and the phone numbers of the women that you don't want to date in your left pocket.

But it was my first time and needless to say I got confused early on and I had a few drinks and I just kept taking these phone numbers and stuffing them everywhere. The good news was I had about 57 dates after this. Some of which I don't even remember. But I took out all of the women.

Anyway I did my best to mingle and introduce myself. And I observed that the women approached the celebrities, the ones they recognized, in a different way. They came up to them asking about their show or for their autograph.

Then after about an hour they begin the auction. They hire two professional auctioneers, you know the kind you see selling race horses and cattle. And it's a pretty fast-paced kind of a deal.

When the auction actually began we all were pretty nervous, even the celebrities I was surprised to find. Even the men that have thousands of women across the country in their fan clubs. So we sat backstage and talked about it.

Needless to say the auction began with all the big hitters, like George Clooney who's a big star here in the US and soon to be a big star all over the place when he does Batman, who went for thousands and thousands of dollars. It was a bidding frenzy of women that were just beside themselves to get a date with George. And then they filter in the other bachelors.

As the night progressed the women reacted in a funny way to some of the men being auctioned. For example, there's this local disc jockey here who calls himself the Nasty Man on KISS radio. And he's a muscular, clean shaven fella. He's on the radio every night talking about sex, relationships and rock 'n' roll. And I thought, here's a guy that would rock the socks off these women. He came out in all black leather and boots and a shirt all torn apart. And the women reacted to him in a different way, they didn't bid high. And he actually got some hecklers in the audience. So, the women were very discerning about who they picked.

When it was time for me to go up, I was nervous and sweating and thinking, 'I am going to be lucky if I get a hundred dollars.' And I was hoping that one of the women in the audience that knew me would just take pity on me. When I came out, I kept most of my clothes on, unlike some of the other bachelors. I think I just took off my jacket. And I got an unbelievable reaction. I was taken by surprise. I walked out onto the stage and hundreds and hundreds of the women who I had met and talked to, rallied to support me. And this bidding frenzy took place that was overwhelming. The women went ballistic. They were screaming and hollering everything, from 'Take it off' and, 'Come over here' to 'Give it to me baby'. I came down the runway, I walked around a little bit, trying to get them to bid even more and come on and help me out. And they went into even more of a frenzy.

Eventually the auctioneers said, 'Let's bring this man down into the audience. Get him down here.' So they brought me down off the stage and as I came down off the stage, one woman who was bidding with all the other women, came up to me and grabbed me and lip-locked me - that's when there's no air between your mouths -

> ## *...there I was in this very passionate kiss with all these women screaming madly.*
>
> GEORGE FALARDEAU

and I felt this device, which I later realized was her tongue, going down my throat and as I pulled back a little bit she pulled my buttocks towards her and wrapped her leg around me. And there I was in this very passionate kiss with all these women screaming madly. And at that point another woman, who ended up winning the date, began a competing bid for me and the bidding got off to an even fiercer pace than before. The woman that kissed me backed off and then the auctioneers pulled me away from her. And I was kind of in a daze.

The final bid was around a couple of thousand dollars. I was one of the top four or five bachelors out of 40, which I was thoroughly pleased with. I was very happy to be able to get that much money and not be embarrassed.

How many of these women did I have sex with? Let's just say some. Not a lot. And I'd like say that I have libido just like anyone else and I am completely heterosexual.

Generally, you're unlikely to get the date of your dreams, or a romance made in heaven followed by marriage at these auctions. But you are going to have a lot of fun.

The lady that selected me at the auction was an outstanding lady and attractive and I can't say enough good things about her. But it wasn't in the cards.

BARBARA DE ANGELIS:
Bachelor auctions and television dating shows are a ridiculous way to find a partner. You may find a date but you're not going to be able to tell anything about that person except that he's attractive or you like his clothes.

ERECTION DRUGS

DOE GENTRY, SINGLES CORRESPONDENT:
Erection drugs? Well, its a shot. You go out on a date and start getting all steamed up and excuse yourself and go to the bathroom and shoot up. They come out and it's up. And I guess sometimes it lasts for four hours.

DR URI PELES, SEX THERAPIST:
Two and a half hours is not the ideal. I think it's up to every individual and his spouse to decide how long they want to make love. My motive here is not to make money for the drug companies but to diminish the amount of medicine needed, reducing it to the minimum effective dose that's right for you or anybody else who's interested in having a satisfying sex life.

And, anyway, what is premature, or what is satisfying sex, or how long should intercourse last - there are all individual questions with individual solutions. Everyone is different.

What you want is an erection that you can rely on so you can have the best sex of your life. I don't see anything wrong with the concept of enrichment and having better sex.

There's no second chance to make a first impression and it would be nice if, the first time, you really come across as a good lover. Women are very forgiving and they understand if you don't function very well the first time, but they definitely remember you if you've been a

> *What you want is an erection that you can rely on so you can have the best sex of your life.*
>
> DR URI PELES

99

good lover the first time around and this can carry you a long way into the relationship.

For the younger man, the major problem is premature ejaculation and we have sex therapy, reconditioning techniques and medication like Serotonin for that. An older person may have a combination of the two problems: premature ejaculation and erection problems. And for the former, we can slow him down with a variety of distracting techniques. But for the latter, the injection is an ideal solution, because he gets two solutions for one problem. I have people coming here of all ages. I have patients of 85 and it's nice to look at those guys and think when I'm 85, I'll be okay. And there are very few words to describe the exhilaration people feel when they see the results they can get.

> ❝ *And there are very few words to describe the exhilaration people feel when they see the results they can get.* ❞
>
> DR URI PELES

CHRIS, MALE ESCORT:
I take a pill called yohambe. It makes your body create natural energy in the groin. So when you do get an erection it's harder and it stays longer. If a person usually has an erection for two hours they'll have one for four hours. And it's basically designed basically for your 70 year old men who can't get a hard on. So if you're only 25 and can get hard and you don't need nothing to help you and you take yohambe, you're gonna be getting real hard and lasting.

BARBARA DE ANGELIS:
I think the idea of erection as king, having to prolong it for ten hours or to be a stud with your 20 year old girlfriend, is ridiculous.

Making love has so much more to do with the heart

than the body. And most women are looking for tender-
ness, compassion, sensitivity and caring and whether or
not the guy lasts ten minutes, five minutes or a half hour,
isn't the issue.

A lot of women tell me, 'I'd rather have him just hold
me and say nice things to me than be a sexual acrobat.'

DR URI PELES:
When you inject the medication it mimics a natural erection. Once you ejaculate, the penis comes down naturally
most of the time and you stop when you don't have the
desire to have sex anymore.

SEYMORE BUTTS, PORN STAR:
I heard that John Bobbit was using these erection injec-
tions to achieve a hard on while he was doing his first
movie after his penis was sliced off and reattached.
However, I don't hear about it in the industry. I know
one guy that has a penis pump so that he can pump it up
at any time, but everybody else I know uses standard
operating procedures.

ADAM WEST:
I've never really believed much in aphrodisiacs. I know
there's a problem now with a certain drug which some
rather nefarious, to use a Batman term, characters are
using on their dates.

> **"A lot of women tell me,
> 'I'd rather have him just hold me
> and say nice things to me than
> be a sexual acrobat.'"**
> BARBARA DE ANGELIS

JOHN, ERECTION DRUG USER:

How do I use an erection drug on a date? Well, before the date, you camouflage the syringe in something. I use a Cuban cigar tube, they're about seven inches long or so and the syringe is only about five inches long and it fits right in there really neat. Then you put the cigar tube in the refrigerator, hidden, like in a low drawer somewhere, so if they're going to your refrigerator behind your back for water, they don't see it. And if anybody did see it, I'd say, 'I keep my cigars fresh that way.'

If I know I'm going to make love, when you're kissing them and the clothes are coming off and you're getting somewhere, you just say, 'Excuse me, I have to go use the restroom for a second'. And they think you're going to clean up and I'll go get some water from the refrigerator and then put the cigar tube in my pocket, go into the restroom, and then do my thing.

I come out and it takes anywhere from five to about fifteen minutes to work. Or it may not work at all. If you went to work after you did that you probably wouldn't get an erection. But once you start kissing and getting sexual, boom, it just comes on real strong, you get very excited, very hard, very erect, as big as you've ever been in your life on this stuff, you're as big as you would ever be, without fail. And so it works very naturally that way, you stay soft until you start kissing and making out and then it just comes up and stays hard for a long time.

> *...once you start kissing and getting sexual, boom, it just comes on real strong...*
>
> JOHN

> " *I think the idea of erection as king, having to prolong it for ten hours or be a stud with your 20 year old girlfriend, is ridiculous.* "
>
> BARBARA DE ANGELIS

SEX CHARMS

NAOMI, SEX CHARM CONSULTANT:
It's kind of innocuous looking. The clip part clips on to your pubic hair and the tail end - no pun intended - touches your clitoris if you're a woman, and the shaft of the penis if you're a man. That part's extremely important. And as you're clipping it on you recite an incantation aloud three times. I always tell people, 'Pretend you're a method actor, feel what you're saying. Because it is about your energy and things that are happening to you.' And each time you say the incantation you say it with greater conviction.

These are custom made sex charms, they're talismans, designed to enhance and magnify the wearer's sexual energy. My partner created them about ten years ago. They're made with a combination of copper and stallion hair. The other ingredients are secret.

LAURA, COMEDY WRITER:
What I found is that, this charm is so intense, you don't always have to be wearing it. After you've taken it off, it can be sitting by the bed and you'll be just, you know, bouncing off walls. People find that, even the first time they wear it, it enhances sex or makes it wild and crazy.

> *...they're talismans, designed to enhance and magnify the wearer's sexual energy.*
>
> NAOMI

NAOMI:

They cost $150 each. That's it. No sliding scale. And, knowing what women spend on make-up, I actually think that's very reasonable.

The first time I wore it I decided I would just make it do what it was intended to do. I thought, I'll just make eye contact with a couple of people across the bar and I did and they started to come over.

And I realized that I really didn't want them to come over. But I did it anyway. And I had a girlfriend with me who was unaware I was wearing it. All she saw were these people hovering around me. I had your proverbial cast of thousands around me. That was night number one. And she finally said, 'I don't know what you're doing but can I have your overflow?'

> *People find that, even the first time they wear it, it enhances sex or makes it wild and crazy.*
> LAURA

SHERRI SPILLANE:

Charms attached to pubic hair? Give me a break! You've gotta be joking.

I think that's a bit much. I'd like to know what these charms look like and if they get in the way. I mean they'd certainly be in the way if you were trying to have oral sex, wouldn't they? Unless they came in different flavours. My God, I thought I'd heard it all! You've really got me on that one.

LAURA:

I'll go out and if I'm eating dinner alone, which I love to do, I'll wear it. And someone will usually send a drink over to me. I wear it when I want to. It's my choice. I don't want to abuse it or overuse it. I think it's a special thing.

Attaching it is no problem because it has this little clip.

It's like clip-on earrings, just in a cuter place. Does it tickle? No, I can't feel a thing.

I'm only going to tell you a little bit of my chant because, you know, I can't trust everyone with it. When I put it on, I say, 'Oh, Stallion, wild stallion, like a wild horse, a sexy horse, you cannot resist me if I want you. So, if I want you to be mine, you will be mine, you do not have a choice. I'm a sexual being from head to toe and from toe to head and you're mine.' And that's as far as I'm going to go because I think it's a personal thing.'

STRANGE SEX

BRENDA LOVE:
Insects are used sometimes in the S&M community. Some use ants or other stinging insects. There was one guy who would cover himself with honey, lie out in his backyard, and ants would crawl all over him and sting him.

There's a group near Los Angeles called Squish Productions. It has about 300 members. These guys are aroused by seeing their significant others step on bugs. These guys don't think about the bugs. They fantasize that they are the bug being squished by huge attractive females. One guy said that when he was a small child, his older sister would play with him and she would be rough, throwing him to the floor and stepping on him or rolling him around with her foot.

I spent some time trying to find out why some people have these strange fetishes, like seeing their partner step on bugs or hitting themselves in the face with a pie or having a prostitute throw oranges at their rear end when they're walking back and forth in a bathtub with high heels or that guy that swallowed those Barbie doll heads. And I discovered that all these fetishes are some sort of imprinting deriving from something that happened to

> *They fantasize that they are the bug being squished by huge attractive females.*
>
> BRENDA LOVE

them when they were young, something that triggered an adrenalin rush from fear or anger or even love.

Take, for example, a shoe fetish. Psychologists say that it usually starts when a toddler or small child crawls over to his or her mother - it could be the father - and the last thing that they see before they're picked up and nurtured and held is that person's shoes or their feet. And so in the mind of a very young child, love and affection comes from that last object they see.

> *There are lots of clubs for different fetishes and lifestyles in LA.*
>
> BRENDA LOVE

There are lots of clubs for different fetishes and lifestyles in LA. There's the swingers' club for people who like to swap partners, there's clubs for people who like to have sex in public, there are even vampire clubs for people who like to consume blood, there's something for everyone.

JEFF VALENCIA, WHO RUNS SQUISH PRODUCTIONS:
Ever since I was a little kid, I've enjoyed women's feet, being stepped on, walked on. In 1991, I made a short film called Squish which was reviewed in an adult foot-fetish paper and I started getting letters.

In fact, in 1991, I probably had a three-ring binder full of letters and today I've got about 40 three-ring binders full of letters. They're from people all over the world talking about what they enjoy and what sort of things they like seeing squished.

There's a variety of things that can be crushed including cockroaches, worms, crickets and it goes all the way up to small vertebrates like mice. I've seen underground videos of small chickens, mice and rats.

When I was a child, I had two older sisters and they would bring their little girlfriends over and go in their room and play and I would go in there and torment them and try to get them to step on me.

It started with a simple foot fetish and then I started thinking, 'Well, what if I was smaller, what if I was bug size' and it just evolved.

> *I have a regular foot fetish,*
> *so I like to lick girls feet. Girls, in general,*
> *taste pretty good.*
>
> JEFF VALENCIA

I'd have to tell the girl right off, you know, which is why I'm so successful at dating. 'Want to come back to my house and crush some bugs?' I love women. I wish I had a girlfriend right now, it'd be kind of nice.

I have a regular foot fetish, so I like to lick girls feet. Girls, in general, taste pretty good. You can lick them just about anywhere. Especially after they've just come back from an aerobics class. Like, real sweat. Real men lick real sweat, you know. Who wants all that perfume anyway?

Generally, as a rule, you can work your way into a girl's shoe. All girls like foot massage, right? Then if

> *Oh, I think*
> *that is totally,*
> *absolutely*
> *revolting.*
>
> BRYCE BRITTON

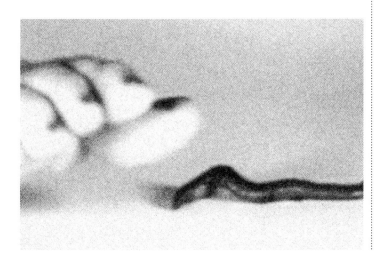

you're really bold, and they've had experience with it before, you might be able to suck on their toes or something like that. Usually, on the first date, you don't bring the bug thing up, you know what I mean? That comes later, you know, after you've had sex with her. You know, when you're lying there, you say, 'Oh, by the way, I have this little box of bugs here somewhere.'

You see, in the mind of the crush freak, he is the bug. The insect is a surrogate, so he's fantasizing that he's actually the one under the foot being squashed. So, it's a foot fetish/mild sado-masochism/humility fetish.

KIM, SAFE SEX PARTY GOER:

Wow, every time is different, but the good thing about the Queen of Heaven party is it has a lot people, 200 people, so there's often a big selection. I'm bisexual so I play with women and men. Intercourse is not something I often do at play parties, just because to me it's a very intimate act. So, I could get into some kind of erotic play with a woman, it just really depends on who's here, how I feel personally. Tonight I'm feeling kind of mellow so I don't feel like getting into some really intense scene. Play parties give you an opportunity to act on your fantasies. Personally, I like being taken by force.

> *Play parties give you an opportunity to act on your fantasies. Personally, I like being taken by force.*
>
> KIM

GERALD, GUEST AT SEX PARTY:

Well, I think the philosophy has to do with encouraging people to feel comfortable with their bodies, to feel comfortable with their sexuality and encourage sexual variation. There's no strict borders of heterosexual, homosexual, male or female or whatever, there's a lot of blending, a lot of experimenting, a lot of playing with boundaries. And the philosophy behind it is that sex is a good thing, that it's positive, that it's healthy, that's it's necessary, that it's something that we all need, that it's a normal part of life and it's a joyous part of life. I know that sounds so pompous, doesn't it? But ... it's fun to come here and get into a big pile and have sex with lots of different people.

TREVOR, GUEST AT SEX PARTY:
So far there has been very little jealousy between me and my partner and that's because I work very hard to make sure there isn't. There would be jealousy if I were sleeping with men, but since I only sleep with women, he deals with that pretty well. I think he knows I'm getting something that he couldn't give me. Anyway he's not into S & M and he knows I'm very much into it so I think he's pleased that I can get that out of my system instead of becoming frustrated and cranky at home. He has said on occasion that when I go off to play parties he does get a little bit anxious, he's afraid that I'll meet somebody that I'll like better than him and I'll leave him. I just work very hard to make sure that he knows that I love him and that this doesn't interfere with our sex life.

And he also sees me running around before sex parties screaming, 'I can't go to this party, I'm too nervous!' and I think that elevates the jealousy quite a bit.

GERALD:
All types of people come to these parties. One thing that I've noticed is that people who come tend to be white and middle class. I don't know what that's about. I don't know if that's a psychological thing or if it's just that those are the only people who can afford to pay $15-$20 to go to a party. Other than that, there's a wide variety of ages, body types, sexual practices, sexual preferences.

In fact, one of the reasons I like The Queen of Heaven parties is that they're so varied. That's the name of the game. There's men, there's women, there's trans-gender people, there's gays, there's straights, there's bisexuals, just a huge variety. I see old people, young people. But they're generally white and middle class.

BRENDA LOVE:

It seems like there are people that swallow either large pieces of food for the choking sensation. And it's probably similar to erotic asphyxiation where people deliberately strangle themselves or their partners to block off the oxygen which triggers the survival mechanism in your body. You panic. You can't breathe. And it releases a lot of endorphines and a lot of adrenalin, both sexually stimulating chemicals.

MONIQUE, SEX SYMBOL DYNASTY GROUP:

Sometimes fans write in asking for our smelly pantyhose. They want us to wear boots all day long and then send them the pantyhose.

Sometimes fans write in asking us for our smelly pantyhose. They want us to wear boots all day long and then send them the pantyhose.

MONIQUE, SEX SYMBOL DYNASTY GROUP

JULIE, SEX SYMBOL DYNASTY GROUP:

They want them in a zip-lock bag, so the smell is preserved. If they're going to pay $100 for a pair of old pantyhose that we're going to throw away, of course we're going to send them to them in the mail. They can have them!

BRENDA LOVE:

In the S&M community you have to learn about safety. You don't want to kill your partner, or injure them. You won't find anyone else to play with if you do.

The S&M community in the United States is estimated by some psychologists to be ten per cent of the population. Kinsey, when he did his research, said that up to 60 per cent of the people he interviewed said that they were aroused by being bitten. Biting is a form of S&M.

The S&M community in the United States is estimated by some psychologists to be ten per cent of the population.

BRENDA LOVE

A lot of the people have their partners whip them. It's sort of like a massage. It makes their back tingle. It reduces stress for some of them.

The ones that have a dungeon will equip it with maybe 20 different paddles, maybe a leather or latex suit. They may have hoods.

They'll have a variety of different whips. Some of them will have a lot of exotic costumes. They may have something from the 1600s or cowboy outfits because it's sort of a theatre, role playing. They don't just spank each other. Some will have a swing hanging from the ceiling or a crucifix that you hang a person on. Sometimes a gynaecology bed or dental chair or a cage. So it could get expensive. Most of them build their own dungeons but still there are a lot of items that you have to buy.

There was a guy that ended up at the San Francisco General Hospital because he had swallowed five or six Barbie doll heads. Usually he would swallow one or two and pass them and boil them and re-swallow them. But

> *There was a guy that ended up at the San Francisco General Hospital because he had swallowed five or six Barbie doll heads.*
>
> BRENDA LOVE

because of the sheer number of heads he swallowed that time, he injured his lower intestine and so he had to go into hospital.

He brought a zip-lock bag with him with two or three of the shaped Barbie doll heads in it so he could show the doctor what he'd done, but they didn't believe him. So they x-rayed his stomach and on the x-ray, which was passed around the whole hospital, (I found out from one of the professors that I lectured to at San José State) you could see these Barbie doll heads in his stomach. So there was proof that he actually did it.

STALKERS

...when it turns from that love into that hate, that's when it becomes very dangerous...

KELLY LANGE

KELLY LANGE, AUTHOR OF
***TROPHY WIVES* AND BROADCASTER:**
I know a lot about stalkers because I've had several. I work at Channel 4 news in Los Angeles. I've been on the air here for 20 years and I'm high profile so my hours are pretty easy to figure out. I do the four o'clock news and the 11 o'clock news. At about midnight, I leave and go home. And I've been followed. I had a stalker who was arrested in front of the station after his employer tipped my employer off. And he was picked up with a handgun, a rifle and ammunition and he served his time.

Well, first of all, he started writing nice letters. I wrote back once, maybe twice. I never write back to a person more than twice. And, usually, they write to get a picture, get some information or whatever. But when they write more than that it becomes something else.

He wrote more until it was three or four times a day and he was sending flowers and gifts. And he started out with, 'I care for you very much', 'I like you' and then, 'I love you' and then it's, 'You bitch, I'm going to kill you". That's the pattern.

I did a lot of research into how they work and that's exactly how mine worked. And when it turns from that love into that hate, that's when it becomes very dangerous.

It's totally unpredictable. You can't say, 'Well, he's going to do this and now he's going to do that' or think logically, 'Don't you think if you do this, he won't do that?' There's no logic to it at all because these people are completely deranged.

It was frightening. I was taking everything he sent and turning it over to my bosses and they were turning it over to the police. But then a postcard arrived and I saw it and he had written on the back, 'I know what time you get off at night and I know what door you come out of, it's just past the Johnny Carson studio, and when you

LIFE ON MARS?

KELLY LANGE

walk out one of these nights, I'm going to shoot you in the head. I'm going to blow your head off and you'll never know what hit you.' Well, that got my attention. It was terrifying. That's when I got security.

Since that time, I look over my shoulder all the time. I am always aware of who's driving behind me. When I walk outside the building, I'm aware of who's around. I wasn't before. I was blithely happy. But it does that to you. It makes you absolutely aware of your environment. I have pepper spray on my key chain and everywhere I walk, I walk with my finger on the trigger. It's legal in California now, before you had to get a license for it. If you push the trigger, it will shoot 15 feet into the air. It will incapacitate someone for 45 minutes with burning and scratching. It won't hurt anybody permanently, it won't kill anybody.

> *Since that time, I look over my shoulder all the time. I am always aware of who's driving behind me.*
>
> KELLY LANGE

I think all women should carry it. I've sent some to my friends. I sent one to Jackie Collins, who's a friend of mine. And she wrote back to me saying, 'Thank's so much for my pepper spray, I can't wait to use it.'

You know, it's funny, when the man sold it to me at the sporting goods store, he said, 'Understand Ms Lange, it's only good for four attacks.' Oh please, I'm not planning on having more than four attacks, thank you. We don't carry guns here. You have to have a permit to carry a gun. But you can have a gun in your house, which is what I do.

Madonna was stalked. When I did the Lisa Gibbons show, one of the questions she asked was, 'Why would Madonna not show up in court? Why was she reluctant to show up? Why did she have to be summoned to show up?'

But, I can relate to Madonna. You don't want to look at the person because you know you're giving him exactly what he wants, which is the attention. And, he's going to be in and out of prison, or perhaps he'll be acquitted and then he could kill you, you know. It's very frightening. Look at Rebecca Shafer. She was stalked. It was easy for that man. He was determined to find out exactly where she lived so he could come and ring her doorbell. And that's what he did and when she answered her doorbell, he shot and killed her.

JOHN, PRIVATE INVESTIGATOR:
We worked for one celebrity woman who had been coming home to her house in the afternoon after filming to find devil worship types running away from the house. She called the police and they found evidence of devil worshipping all over her property. And as it was coming up to Easter, which is a big devil-worshipping time, she hired us to be on her property one night. At 4am we caught them on the property.

The majority of celebrity stalkers have no intentions of hurting the star. But they're so disruptive in the star's life and they're so dedicated to being in the star's life that it's a major problem for the celebrity and we have to stop it right away.

CHRISTINE O'KEEFE, BEVERLY HILLS MATCHMAKER:
Stalking is a pretty serious topic, it's certainly one that frightens a lot of people. It's been very well publicized that many celebrities are stalked.

Some of the most famous are David Letterman and Mary Lou Henner. Madonna was stalked, my God, she was nearly killed. The man almost succeeded in getting to her. It's frightening.

When you're in the public eye, whatever you're well known at, whether your in show business or a successful attorney or doctor, there is most likely someone out there that maybe just doesn't have it all together.

> *The majority of celebrity stalkers have no intentions of hurting the star.*
>
> JOHN

JACKIE COLLINS:

When you consider that most actresses today take their clothes off, as they're in *Playboy* magazine, they're in the movies, they're showing everything, I mean that guy in the street, that guy who's obsessed with them, he thinks, 'Well, she has no secrets from me, I know what she looks like naked, I can go for her, she's mine!'

PHYLLIS DILLER:

Being stalked is very dangerous situation for stars, especially female stars where men are stalking them and in several cases there have been deaths. I'm really not concerned with stalking because most of my stalkers would have walkers and canes.

> **Well, she has no secrets from me,**
> **I know what she looks like naked,**
> **I can go for her, she's mine!**
> JACKIE COLLINS

My only problem has been through the mail. I had a little bit of stalking through the mail. Men become too possessive and write too often and you begin to wonder just what's wrong with them.

Taking action is dangerous. You have to just try and get the message through to them that your communicating with them is a very impersonal thing.

ALEXANDRA PAUL:

It's funny 'cause I get a lot of fan mail at my house, I get fan mail at my house from Germany, from Japan. I don't know how they get my address, but they get it. I do not respond to anything that comes to my home.

JULIE:

Shortly after I became a *Penthouse* Pet I had gone to bed early on a Saturday night and I woke up to find a man standing over my bed with a screw driver at my throat. And I had to fight this guy with hand-to-hand combat and literally throw him out of my house. And if I wasn't six foot one and as strong as I am I probably would have been attacked, raped and maybe even killed by this guy.

I have a really strong feeling about what we do for our fans. We give something back and we make ourselves available. We will sign pictures and send them to our fans. It gives them a piece of what they are hungry for and they need that. People like Demi Moore and Andie McDowell and Sharon Stone never make themselves available and that kind of pisses the fans off and they get angry and want to stalk. They just want to have that moment with you. So we make ourselves available to meet.

RHONDA, SEX SYMBOL DYNASTY GROUP:

You don't know what it is in the mind of a fan or someone who adores you. There might be more than one screw missing. I got this letter from this man who sent back my picture torn up. This guy had seen me on a television show talking about a date and he wrote to me and said, 'How could you break off our wedding plans this way? I've saved $600 and it is in my cookie jar and I am going to marry you and then you hurt me this way'. This was a little scary. Because this guy was having his own little love affair. And you really don't know what can happen. And then they turn up on your doorstep.

GENA LEE NOLIN:

I was working on *The Price is Right*, which is a big, big game show in the US, and I was working with CBS and for the first time ever in their mail department I received a knife from a man who threatened my life, saying that if he couldn't date me or be with me or something crazy that he was going to kill me.

STEPHANIE BEACHAM:

Don't get paranoid, but do get careful. You really do

I woke up to find a man standing over my bed with a screwdriver at my throat.

JULIE

have to, particularly in town, you've got to be very careful that your address is not known. It's a real worry. I've had people who have written and in the end, because of the nature of the sort of stuff they were writing, I had to inform the police so that if anything should happen, if I'm found in a bloody pile, they'll know it could be that guy that did it. But then there's a balance isn't there?

ALEXANDRA PAUL:
If I had a stalker it would be very scary. Privacy is a very important thing and people shouldn't have to deal with fear in their home. I would do anything to avoid it. I'd move if there was a stalker.

SWINGERS AND SAFE SEX

DIANE CONWAY:
Swinging is when two or more different couples get together and do it with each other's partner. I'm way too jealous for that. Way too jealous. I want to be with one person at a time and I'm not really interested in looking at somebody else's equipment, you know. I mean, if you've seen enough penises in your life, you've seen enough. You don't need to see lots more, they look alike. They're kind of ugly anyway.

Swinging is never helpful. It's unnatural, it's not going to help anybody. It is going to bring up insecurities in everybody there. Because you're always comparing your insides to somebody else's outsides. You're going to say, 'Oh my God, her boobs are bigger than mine, her hair doesn't have black roots, mine does and look at those eyelashes!' And he's going to compare, 'Oh, look at his physique'. It's not good.

> *I'm way to jealous for that. I want to be with one person at a time and I'm not really interested in looking at somebody else's equipment, you know.*
> DIANE CONWAY

BRENDA LOVE:
They say that sexually transmitted diseases are very rare among swingers and they don't know of any cases where a person has got AIDS.

SHERRI SPILLANE:
I don't like people who swing. I think it's a sickness. What you're getting into is not people who have a real desire for one another, it's just people who go to total strangers and indulge in sex.

If there's no desire for another person on an intellectual or sexual basis then it's just sex for sex's sake and what does that mean? These are people who are probably sexually addicted, their lives are not exciting enough so they try to get the excitement by doing that, but I think it's pretty sad.

ROGER CLINTON:
You know, that's another thing that I just can't understand. But I do have to admit - no names announced here - I know a few people, I have a few friends, that are like that. I was even approached once about it.

> *I just don't feel like sharing myself or my spouse.*
> ROGER CLINTON

"We generally find it's the man who has the greater interest at first and he has to do some talking to get his wife to come along.

STEVE MASON

I mean, I live in Hollywood, and I've been street smart for many many years, and I've been around the block a few times, but I'm just old-fashioned. I'm convinced about certain things and one of them is the institution of marriage and about being one on one. I just don't feel like sharing myself or my spouse.

I had plenty of years of swinging. There was a different definition of swinging then, it didn't have to do with married couples. Now swingers are married couples that swap. I had plenty of years of diversity and I am quite satified with the way my life has changed and where I am right now. I don't care to share or be shared.

STEVE MASON, MEMBER AND ORGANIZER, THE LIFESTYLES ORGANIZATION:

The Lifestyles Organization started 23 years ago and it has expanded. It started as a swingers' group, but now we attract lots and lots of mainstream couples who simply want to come in and get a little bit of excitement and romance into their lives.

A swingers' group is a place where people go and perhaps share partners or perhaps get into an orgy. We have the world's largest couples' convention where couples get together simply to enjoy the sexy costumes, the dances, the seminars, the idea of being with other people who are sexually liberated.

We generally find it's the man who has the greater interest at first and he has to do some talking to get his wife to come along. We're a no-pressure kind of society here so that when people come they blend in.

But, after a very short period of time, the women get involved because it's empowering for a woman to be able to wear something that's very sexy, very revealing and have everybody look at her and say, 'Gee, that's very nice', as opposed to wearing it in a shopping centre where people would look and say, 'You're going to frighten the horses'.

At our conventions we get thousands of people from

around the world, so it happens occasionally that somebody there gets sore at a spouse. But it's amazing that with that many people it happens very infrequently. It's a very happy, loving, supportive group. People are not denied, they're not frustrated, they're not fixated, so they're all having a good time.

It's interesting that there's not an awful lot of drinking. There's practically no drug use. Everybody there is into it and jealousy is not much of a problem. I think people here feel that you don't share love, but you can share sex.

We don't worry about people wearing condoms and we don't worry about safe sex because if sex kills, it heals a billion times more often. Generally speaking, sex is one of the safest things you can do and I think it really is our puritanical attitude that's the problem. We expect sex to be dirty. We expect sex to cause problems. But, in fact, sex is really quite safe.

> *You would generally have some trouble with single males coming along, trying to grab. They were like kids in a candy store.*
>
> STEVE MASON

The conventions used to be open to singles but you would generally have some trouble with single males coming along, trying to grab and they would just be overly aggressive. They were like kids in a candy store. And so, we started to make it couples only and all of our members have responded very enthusiastically. The only time when we have an odd number is if we have a legitimate triad, which is two males and one female, and they actually live together, or two females and one male. And there are a few of those, but not very many.

I got involved when I was a lot younger and I wanted to try different females. My wife was a little hesitant at first, but then she went along with it and found that she enjoyed it as much as I did. I came across the group when they invited me to give a talk. I thought were a health-food organization group and I was going to talk about, you know, living longer and taking vitamins and that sort of thing. But then I found out it was a swingers' group and I saw how happy the people were, I started to come and soon after, my wife joined me and we're very much a part of the group now. We like the social aspect.

GEORGE, MEMBER, THE LIFESTYLES ORGANIZATION:
I have some firm rules about being a member. I never go with a lady unless I know her husband. And, incidentally, I always thank him after I've been with her so that he knows for sure that I've been with her - I don't want him slipping up behind me and knocking me on the head and saying, 'Ooh, I just found out". You know, I want him to know right away.

KITTY FOX, PORN STAR:
I've only ever seen fights at swing parties a few times. Occasionally new couples leave the party in a huff because one of them gets jealous. But true swingers have a good time and they may party with other couples or they may not. Sometimes they just like to socialize.

KIM, SAFE SEX PARTY GOER:
I'm been a monitor at this party, you often get two or three roving monitors, they're people who are well trusted by Carol and Robert, the host and hostess.

Our job is to make sure all genital contact is done with a latex glove, all sex is done with condoms, even oral. Its pretty strict.

I think people are extra cautious because this is such an AIDS centre and there are a lot of people who are HIV positive in this city. And it's interesting, there was some research done about two years ago and the statistics for HIV positive people within play parties is relatively small, which blows me away.

> *I never go with a lady unless I know her husband.*
>
> GEORGE

People have to sign a safe sex waiver before they can enter the party, so they understand the rules. You can't touch anybody unless you ask permission. Coming to play parties is really good for learning to set boundaries.

Swingers are often very married people, getting together with other very married couples, who have maybe outlived the fun of their marriage. The married people I've met who do this kind of thing, seem a little bit conservative in some ways, it's very vanilla, you know, basic sex play.

RICHARD, GUEST AT SEX PARTY:

I've been monogamous for 12 years primarily because of AIDS. The outbreak of the epidemic coincided with the birth of children, so I wasn't predisposed to want to cat around very much anyway with new babies in the house and the kind of bond that exists between a man and a woman at that time. But now the babies are 10 and 12 and 14 and it seems like I could use a night out. And the wife said to me, 'Okay, just practise safe sex', so that's what I'm doing and it's great.

> *...we needed to get away from 'if it isn't intercourse it isn't real sex'.*
>
> NINA HARTLEY

BARBARA DE ANGELIS:

When you talk about morality in Hollywood, you really have to break down the entertainment community by age. If you look at, for instance, the 50-plus age group, maybe pre-AIDS, they would have been divorced and played around and had all kinds of girlfriends or all kinds of boyfriends. It's not like that now. These days if they get divorced they're probably going to get married again. They find somebody and they settle down again. They don't want to sleep around.

The 40-somethings, if you notice, are all married and having babies or they're single and having babies or they're adopting babies. The idea of dating doesn't even relate to them and I know many actresses in their late '30s and '40s who are celibate. They're just not seeing anybody, they're not even interested, they just want to have a family life. The 20-somethings are divided into two groups: there's the crazy kind of druggy/music industry people and they may indeed still be having sex and not caring about AIDS, and then there are the others who are very serious, very career minded, they want to have a family and they're looking at the old brat packers and realizing they don't want to end up like that and they're taking their careers and their personal lives very seriously.

So that's kind of an overview of the Hollywood morality.

NINA HARTLEY:

In our culture sex is intercourse. Everything else is not the real thing or it's not good enough. But HIV has opened up all kinds of other behaviour: dancing, massage, body rubbing, mutual masturbation, erotic talk, voyeurism, exhibitionism and all kinds of other things that are sexually pleasurable.

And we needed to get away from 'if it isn't intercourse it isn't real sex'. There are lots of ways to share orgasm that are completely safe and do not endanger your health or lead to pregnancy.

SEX SURROGATES

BRYCE BRITTON:

A sex surrogate is a trained professional who becomes the partner of a client. She will take him through a series of sensory, sensual, sexual and communicative exercises, and during that process, establishes a relationship with that individual within professional boundaries. There is always a therapist involved in that relationship between the partner and the client.

JACKIE COLLINS:

Sex surrogates were very big in the '80s. I think they kind of phased out in the '90s because of AIDS. But it would be a way of a guy having an affair and being able to say to his wife, 'But sweetheart, this is therapy.'

BRYCE BRITTON:

Many different types of individual can benefit from surrogate work. First of all, there are those who lack social skills or who have a lack of experience in communicating, both verbally and non-verbally with someone of the opposite sex. Then there are men who aren't able to contain arousal, also known as early ejaculation. They get so excited that it's over before they get going and their partners can become angry about that. A surrogate's work is especially important in those cases because she can teach the client to hold onto his energy, to spread out his sensual and sexual feelings through his whole body and, as he goes through the series of exercises, he will become more comfortable with pleasure.

In issues of potency, or when a man ages, the client will often have a picture in their mind of the way they want to be, which is a 20 or 30 year old but their body has changed. And surrogate work teaches people about how their sexuality changes as they age.

> *It would be a way of a guy having an affair and being able to say to his wife, 'But sweetheart, this is therapy.'*
>
> JACKIE COLLINS

Of course, there's a real fine line between prostitution and people becoming dependent on a sex therapist.

BARBARA DE ANGELIS

Well, the relationship between the client and the surrogate can definitely get physical. It starts off by just touching. By the fourth session, you usually have a session called body image and you take your clothes off and talk about your body. Then you move into non-demanding, pleasuring exercises. And from a back caress, you move to front caress, where the genitals are excluded, and from there to front caress, casually including the genitals, but not focusing on them. Then you actually look at each other's genitals and start getting more comfortable and then maybe move into a shower. They're still just touching at this point, sensually all over the body. Following that you move to an exercise called the quiet vagina where, with a limp penis, a man becomes comfortable with what it's like to be inside a woman's vagina and then into masturbation exercises. And after that you move on into intercourse.

JACKIE COLLINS:

There was one particular therapist - a very famous therapist - who would make you take off all your clothes so that he could see the tension points. Yeah, sure!

SUKI, SEX SURROGATE:

We move on to the face and on to the feet and we start taking our clothes off and getting more intimate and more comfortable with each other's bodies. We've been taught not to touch but most of the time, if we ask for permission, people usually will say, 'Yeah, okay', or 'No, I'm not comfortable with that but ask me in a couple of hours and I might be. I just need more time to relax".

So, I always ask if it's okay to do something. Most of the time, people say, 'Oh yeah, please do, I thought you'd never ask.'

BART, SUKI'S CLIENT:

It has helped me a great deal, because in working with Suki I've discovered that the techniques of being intimate with a person are still there. It was good because I went through a period where I was struggling with opening up and I knew when I was working with Suki that I would be accepted even if I stumbled. If I was having difficulty, she was there to lead me through it and it is a very accepting, very caring environment.

I think that it's been a good thing. I think that I waited too long. I spent a long time thinking about whether or not it was the right thing for me. If I had gone earlier I would've been where I am at now a lot earlier. It is really important for me to get the message across to people that this is a good thing. I talk to a lot of guys and tell them they really shouldn't be afraid of doing this. The levels of awareness and even spirituality open up when you go through this kind of training.

SEX SEMINARS

LOU PAGET, CREATOR OF SEXUALITY SEMINARS:
Sexuality seminars are seminars for hands-on instructions into technique and information on oral and manual sex. The age range of people who've been in the seminar, has gone from 19 to 63. Executives from top companies, Emmy award-winning actresses, the top people. I mean, if I were to say the names you would recognize them.

Why do people come to my seminars? I don't know what motivates them, I don't know whether they come because they want to save a relationship or because they want to have fun. I don't know why they show up. What I tell you about is how I present the seminars and my attitude towards them. They're not about having power over men, they're not about enslaving some man because you're so good at this. No technique, like no outfit, is going to be the one thing that is going to keep you happy or someone else happy. It may work, in the way that a fabulous body works, for about six weeks but that's all. The reason that people want information is because they

I wish someone had sat me down and told me how to do oral sex the right way.

JOAN RIVERS

*They're not about having power over men,
they're not about enslaving some man
because you're so good at this.*

LOU PAGET

want to be able to share it. If someone is using it to have control over someone else, I don't know why they're coming because I make it clear that for me it is about providing respectful, accurate information that validates their own experiences and is safe for them.

Do men find this course intimidating? Some do and some are fascinated by it. That's how the men's seminar got created, the men said, 'Listen, you're doing this for women, you have got to do this for us.'

Women tend to be more open about sharing their experiences but they don't go to that really special, sharing level until they come to something like this seminar. But if women have few places to go, men have even fewer.

What's an average penis size? Well, I've had a range of penises in my life. What they tell you in magazines is that six to seven inches is the average. But guess who wrote those articles? Men. In a recent study at the University of California it was found that the average size of a man's penis is five and a quarter inches by two and three quarters around.

I had a male friend, who's not gay, but who wanted to try putting on a condom the way I teach the women in my seminars, with their mouths. He said, 'Okay, show me. Let me see how easy this is to do.' And I didn't cheat, I didn't give him the eight-inch, I gave him the normal six. He put it in his mouth, I showed him how, and he got so far and he starts coughing, and he says, 'Oh my God how do women do this?' He said he had so much respect for what women who do what he has just gone through. And I said, like anybody else, they have to learn. He said that he will never think of this in the same way again.

JOAN RIVERS:

There are wonderful classes out there for women on flirting, how to catch that man, how to keep a man, how to be good in bed, they're wonderful things.

I wish someone had sat me down and told me how to do oral sex the right way. Men are taken to whore houses. Fernando Llamas said his father took him to a whore who broke him in and told him how to be a great lover. A man I go out with told me that his father took him to prostitutes who showed him what to do to please a woman. Those were different times. Nobody ever took a woman and showed her how to please a man. Therefore it takes you 15, 20 years, before you can say to a girlfriend, 'Can I ask you something?' I think these classes are wonderful.

> " *it isn't technique that's going to do it for you, but the freedom to communicate about it. These seminars will enable you to talk about it.* "
>
> LOU PAGET

Nobody ever told me anything. I have one friend who is very sexy. Once she got them, men never left her. After I'd been married for eight years, I thought maybe she knows something I don't and we sat down at lunch one day and I said, 'I want to know every trick that you do.' And that was just some lunch, and I walked away saying, 'Gee, at least I've been on the right track.' But I also walked away saying, 'Gotta try this, gotta try that.' I was delighted. And I took my daughter, who is 25 years old, to see her godmother and said, 'I am not going to tell it to her. I can't. I wish I could. So will you please take her to lunch and give her the following tips?' And she did and I think that's great.

The worst thing in the world is for someone to sleep with you and walk away going 'Hmm, not worth the sandwich.' That would kill me.

CHAPTER THREE

The Hollywood Dream

MARRIAGES AND WEDDINGS

" Goldie Hawn and Kurt Russell – they adore each other

JACKIE COLLINS

"

Goldie Hawn, actress.

INTRODUCTION

Hollywood weddings are very extravagant.

JACKIE COLLINS

Weddings are a very big deal in LA. All that surgery, all that dieting, the image counselling, the dating agency fees, the endless trips to the hair salon - they've all paid off. You've found your mate. In Hollywood it may well not be a mate for life, but, for now anyway, everything is looking good, so why not celebrate in style. Or, at least, spend thousands of dollars on a lavish wedding.

You want rose petals strewn across the marital bed and gardenias floating in the bathtub? How about a ballroom sunk into your lawn, swathed in acres of silk? Or a song performed by a famous artiste as you walk down the aisle? All this and much, much more can be yours. Simply call the wedding co-ordinators, express your heart-felt desires, write a formidable cheque and it will be done.

Colin Cowie, one of Hollywood's most exclusive co-ordinators, explains how it all adds up: 'It's hair, make-up, gown, clothing, food, press, security, waiters, thank-you notes, invitations, service, flowers, honeymoon arrangements - you go through chequebooks very quickly.'

If this is all too much, head for Vegas where you can get married at a booth without even stepping out of your car. And it will only cost you $30. Or dress up as Ivanhoe and Gwenevere (the medieval look is *very* big at the moment) and get hitched at the Divine Madness Fantasy Wedding Chapel. In Vegas, you can have the wedding you've always dreamed of without disturbing the bank balance. There's everything from chains and bull-whips to Elvis lookalikes singing 'Love Me Tender' as you head for the altar. Charlotte Richards, who runs the Little White Wedding Chapel, once processed 224 weddings in one 24-hour period, but then it was Valentine's Day in Vegas. Some individuals make a hobby out of getting married: Scotty, 88, has just embarked on his 29th marriage! Yet many are still optimistic and the notion of a successful marriage, a lasting relationship, is held dear.

EXTRAVAGANT WEDDINGS

JULIA VERDIN, PRODUCER:
Typical Hollywood weddings are usually very glitzy. The bride will be in an outrageous sort of fairy-tale wedding dress, beautiful flowers in the church, all the little brides-maids dressed in matching colours, fireworks, fountains, everything tends to be very lavish and over the top.

COLIN COWIE, WEDDING CO-ORDINATOR:
Our weddings start at about $50,000 and go up to in excess of $3.5 million in a day. I don't think that's extravagance. I think it's taste. To do things beautifully and tastefully costs a lot of money. I don't think spending a lot of money necessarily equates extravagance if it's done tastefully. I mean, extravagance really went with the '80s. '80s weddings about display and show. In the '90s, it's more about understatement where taste obviously prevails.

We did a wedding for a client last year in a very beautiful ranch in Malibu. Glitzy it was not, but I guess it was extravagant. It was certainly glamorous. The setting was just pristine, it looked like the English countryside with these green rolling lawns. And we did a very, very beautiful ceremony with 77 musicians from the Los Angeles Philharmonic and The Chieftains from Ireland for the cocktail hour. We had Imperial Beluga caviar with big magnums of '76 Tattinger champagne, the last available on the planet. And we had 275,000 roses flown in from Ecuador, all in full bloom, 23,000 yards of silk, antique furniture, beautiful beyond belief. It's the most beautiful thing I think we've - I've - ever created.

We had a very sumptuous and lavishly decorated structure with a sunken dance floor and a ballroom. We had windows draped completely so you got a sense of an indoors and an outdoors rather than the feeling of being confined to the inside of the tent. And we dug down and created a sunken dance floor.

> *...everything tends to be very lavish and over the top.*
>
> JULIA VERDIN

And then, after dinner, we had Tony Bennett, followed by Bruce Springsteen, Billy Joe, Sheryl Crow and Jackson Brown. And we finished it with Jack Mack and the Heart Attack at 3:30 in the morning with breakfast. It was the most unbelievable party.

JACKIE COLLINS:
Hollywood weddings are incredibly extravagant. They feel they've got to outdo maybe Michael Jackson's and Elizabeth Taylor's weddings.

SHERRI SPILLANE, SCANDAL AGENT:
I think extravagant weddings are pointless because lots of people go through a divorce straight afterwards. And then you've thrown all this money away on a bunch of people who probably don't even appreciate it.

Look at the Royal wedding. It was lovely to watch but how much did it cost? And look at it now, it's just a memory in a scrap book. It's on celluloid to last forever, but it cost the country a fortune. I don't see the point in

it. When I got married I ran away and eloped and I would do it again. I would never have an extravagant wedding.

If people want to do that, that's fine, if it makes them happy. But at least I don't have to look back on it and think, 'Oh God, I spent all that money and that son of a bitch walked out on me.'

And we had 275,000 roses flown in from Ecuador, all in full bloom, 23,000 yards of silk, antique furniture, beautiful beyond belief.

COLIN COWIE

JACKIE COLLINS:
I went to a wedding the other day where, as they said, 'I do' a box was opened and out flew dozens of white doves. Where are these poor doves going to go? Lost in the smog of Hollywood!

CELEBRITY WEDDINGS

JACKIE COLLINS:
The smartest celebrities run off and get married on a beach somewhere.

JENNIFER LOFTFIELD, WEDDING CO-ORDINATOR:
Celebrity weddings are always fun. They're always a bit more of a challenge because you're dealing with more security and secrecy. One of the best weddings I did was for Slash of Guns and Roses. He had a really nice wedding but we had a lot of paparazzi to contend with and a lot of newspapers trying to get pictures and so on. I thought with the reputation that Guns and Roses have, it was going to be a really unruly crowd but I have to say they were pretty much on their best behaviour.

COLIN COWIE:

When I did Kenny G's wedding, he had an album out called *Breathless*. On that album is a song called 'The Wedding Song', and it was played as his bride, Lindy, walked down the aisle. It's a most unbelievably beautiful piece of music. When I saw my waiters with tears rolling down their cheeks, I knew that he had written something very special.

> *Celebrity marriages don't last because celebrities are all in a profession where image is more important than being a real person.*
>
> GEORGE ROMAN

KELLY LANGE, AUTHOR OF *TROPHY WIVES*:

What do celebrity weddings cost? Elizabeth Taylor's was certainly a multi-million dollar wedding. By the way, Michael Jackson paid for it. No wonder they're such good friends. He paid for her wedding. That was nice of him, don't you think?

COLIN COWIE:

When you're working with a celebrity, privacy is of paramount importance. And because nobody can know what's going on it makes it very difficult. It's double the amount of service, double the amount of time. We have to go and visit them on location. They're very demanding people.

Because of the paparazzi, we have to apply pseudonyms. I mean, my chef, who has been with me for seven years, he didn't even know who we were working for on the last wedding.

We keep it very private because you can plan a gorgeous garden wedding out on a ranch in Malibu and you end up with three helicopters overhead, which means you'll never hear the Ave Maria.

DR RACHEL COPELAN,
COUPLES COUNSELLOR AND HYPNOTHERAPIST:
People in Hollywood don't always know the meaning of love, or even good sexuality, but they know the meaning of publicity.

DENNIS FRANZ, ACTOR, *NYPD BLUE*:
One of the solutions that I heard about to discourage helicopters from coming in is to have these big weather balloons, helium-inflated balloons, over the area. But then, apparently, the wind from the helicopters blows the balloons away anyway so it doesn't seem to do any good. I did hear about one interesting solution, but I don't know if it worked. Whoopi Goldberg - and I don't know if it was for a wedding or just some formal thing that she was throwing - knew that helicopters were going to come and prepared for them by writing some significant message on the top of her roof where she was having the affair, indicating what they could do with themselves.

> "*Another deterrent is to have these huge balloons at 500, 700 and 1000 feet. And we can release them... it's like a shotgun and a bird in the sky, a helicopter and a balloon.*"
> COLIN COWIE

COLIN COWIE:
I organize a few deterrents. If we're working outdoors, it could be trellis, it could be chiffon, it could be under trees, so that there's no direct viewpoint from above for a camera. Then there's no point in a helicopter being up in the air. Another deterrent, which is real fun, is to have these huge balloons, big tube balloons filled with helium, tethered at 500, 700 and 1000 feet. And we can release them when we need to. And you know, it's like a shotgun and a bird in the sky, a helicopter and a balloon.

People, photographers, go to great lengths, it's hysterical. They've dug themselves into holes in gardens and put bunny rabbit ears on, and disguised themselves with treetops like something out of Platoon or one of those movies. And I've heard of people drilling holes through walls at bachelor parties and trying to hear what's going on on the other side. But we bring in dogs, we have guards on motorbikes, we have people doing patrolling around the property.

A great way to foil people if we're doing a major celebrity wedding is to send out invitations with the date and time but not the address. Once the guest has replied, we have a detailed package couriered to them the day before the wedding with directions on how to get there.

Whoopi Goldberg... knew that helicopters were going to come and she prepared for them by writing some significant message on the top of her roof indicating what she thought they could do with themselves.

DENNIS FRANZ

WEDDING CO-ORDINATORS AND WEDDING TRENDS

GINA LEE NOLIN, ACTRESS, *BAYWATCH*
Wedding co-ordinators are a must. I'm telling you. Because you're so stressed and you want everything to be perfect. I think having someone to organize it for you if you can is wonderful.

COLIN COWIE:
A wedding co-ordinator is someone who's employed by the family or the bride to take care of all the details and arrangements, like following up on the caterer, the flowers, the clothes, the hair, the church, making sure that the limousines are taken care of, and the make-up artists arrive on time, things like that.

The reason people work with me is, either they have a lot of money and they want to do something incredibly tasteful and they don't have the time to do it themselves. Or, they've made a lot of money, and it's first time round money, and they need the wedding to appear tasteful, so it looks like it's old money.

No two weddings that I have ever done ever looked alike. What I would do first is I'd find out from the client where they like to eat, what their favourite restaurants are, where they take vacations, what are their pet hates, what are their favourite colours, what are their likes, what are their dislikes, and based upon that information, I go and design something.

I once had a client I couldn't get any information out of. But her favourite movie was *The Age of Innocence*. So I said, "I hope you've got the budget to go with it" because, of course, we recreated part of *The Age of Innocence*. And, what with everything, the props, flowers, lighting and hair, make-up, gown, clothing, food, press, security, waiters, thank-you notes, invitations, service,

> *Planning a wedding is like producing a movie.*
>
> COLIN COWIE

honeymoon arrangements, it all adds up very quickly, you spend money, you go through chequebooks.

The thing with America, where the divorce rate is one of the highest in the world, is that the main table ends up huge. There's four main tables because you've got the first mother, the second mother and the third mother and it's the same thing on the groom's side.

Recently I designed this very beautiful wedding and then I said to the bride, 'Show me your gown' and when I saw it I said, 'Oh no, honey, you ain't walking down the aisle in that.' That's why we get involved from the very beginning because it's a question of the whole look: the gown, the hair, the make-up, everything.

And the first thing the bride does is she goes off and buys the gown. She doesn't know whether she's getting married indoors or outdoors, and it's a real mistake. There's a different chronology involved as to what to do first. You find the date, then you find the place and then you buy the gown. But style is never really related to money. Just because you have a lot of money, it doesn't mean you're going to pick a nice gown.

Planning a wedding is like producing a movie. With a movie, you have take one, take two, take three. But, when you've got 500 guests there, there's no second chance.

Being designers, we encourage and inject a lot of romance into the ceremony. Like, we'll say to the groom, 'You know, the bride really needs a little pair of drop diamond earrings and if you go and purchase them while she's getting dressed, we'll deliver them to her on a velvet pillow with a little bit of baby's breath and a little love note.' And then we'll tell the bride to do the same thing and buy him a pair of vintage cufflinks to go with a little love letter that's read to him while she's getting changed. So there's many little touches in our arrangements. On the groom's behalf, we'll go into the honeymoon suite and make it ankle deep with rose petals and we'll light one candle for every guest who attended the wedding. And we'll put silk pajamas on the pillows, not that they use them, and gardenias floating in the bathtub and champagne. They're all wonderful things to inject romance into a fabulous evening.

AVRON AND LISA ANSTEY
WHO ARE PLANNING THEIR WEDDING:
We picked Colin [Cowie] because of his absolutely wonderful and amazing style. My mom has great taste as well, she's very creative and very talented in that way and she wanted to work with somebody that was so much better than her. Somebody that could take what she can do to the next level.

> *It'll make you crazy and it'll ruin your life and by the end of it, you won't be able to stand the guy.*
> KELLY LANGE

KELLY LANGE:
Weddings are huge business here. I've done TV series on weddings and they always get high ratings. People love them. And wedding co-ordinators are integral to planning a wedding today because in Hollywood, or in America in general, planning a wedding has become a huge, monumental task. It's no longer a question of mum and daughter pulling all the arrangements together. There's an immense amount of work that needs to be co-ordinated and somebody needs to take care of it. I've always equated planning a wedding with producing a small movie.

We have a wedding chapel in LA where you just make an appointment, you show up, it takes five minutes. We filmed there and people came in wedding gowns, the whole nine yards, or t-shirts and cut-off jeans or whatever, and they marry them one after another.

They bring their own music, they have witnesses, they have rings, they have everything you want. You can come, get married and go. Or you can do your wedding from now until within an inch of your life. You can go from soup to nuts and plan every bit of it and it'll take you a year and a half and it'll make you crazy and it'll ruin your life and by the end of it, you won't be able to stand the guy. But people do that here.

JENNIFER LOFTFIELD:
As a wedding co-ordinator, I do a lot of different things. Some brides I work with on the whole wedding process, from the day she's engaged, to helping her pick her wedding professionals throughout the wedding process, to going to all the meetings with the professionals, helping her pick her flowers, her dress, her tablecloths, the menu. And of course I'm there on the day of the rehearsal to either help at the church or, if the wedding is taking place at a hotel or in a backyard, then I'll run the rehearsal. I'll be there the whole day of the wedding, from the time hair and make-up starts first thing in the morning through the pictures, through the ceremony, through the reception, to the very end of the day when you need to make sure that everything ends up back in its proper place.

The weddings I do probably between $20,000 and $60,000. The most expensive wedding I've ever done was probably around $200,000. Yet I know someone else who's done a £2.5 million wedding, so, really. I'd say the sky's the limit.

I think the trend for weddings in the '90's is that people really want to make the wedding very personal. They still want to keep weddings traditional, with the correct etiquette but they want to bring to it a sense that it's their own wedding. People love to have a wedding in a backyard or in a restaurant, rather than a hotel, or if they do have a wedding in a hotel, they like to bring personal touches to it. I'm seeing more cocktail napkins or little candy boxes or special matchboxes with the bride's and groom's names printed on.

Cigars are the trendiest thing happening right now.

COLIN COWIE

COLIN COWIE:

Cigars are the trendiest thing happening right now. They're very Hollywood. So I serve cigars and we might have cigar rollers to roll cigars for the guests. What ever we do, we like to have the best as far as quality is concerned.

JENNIFER LOFTFIELD:

I think romance certainly exists in Los Angeles. I think people search it out more here, the fairy-tale romance. And I see a lot of romance brought into weddings. There's a trend for releasing butterflies at the ceremony. And there are some very sweet personal touches, like reading out a poem that the bride or the groom has written or telling a story about the couple's engagement.

In LA, people do try to keep up with the Joneses when they marry. And the more elaborate, the more detailed weddings get, the more help people need.

Most of the weddings I see range from around $20,000 to $60,000. It's very difficult in Los Angeles to do a wedding for much less than that if you want all the elements such as photography, dinner, music and so on.

LAS VEGAS

BARBARA DE ANGELIS,
MARRIAGE COUNSELLOR AND THERAPIST:
Oh God, Las Vegas is a big cartoon. It's a bizarre place. It's just like a constant assault on the senses. It's like a big video game spread out in one place. It's a place where a lot of people from Hollywood make money, but it's not the chosen place for the entertainment community to go. In fact, most of the time when you hear us talk among Hollywood people it's like, 'Oh I have to go to Vegas for a convention' or, 'I have to go because one of my clients is there.' But when people from Hollywood take vacations they don't head for Las Vegas.

> *...of all the place in the world, I can't imagine why anyone would ever want to get married in Las Vegas, Nevada.*
> BARBARA DE ANGELIS

I don't think quickie marriages anywhere are a good idea. And, of all the place in the world, I can't imagine why anyone would ever want to get married in Las Vegas, Nevada.

CHARLOTTE RICHARDS, MINISTER:
Our fee at the Little White Wedding Chapel is $45 and that includes the use of the chapel, a candlelit service, music and of course we provide the minister to perform the ceremony for you. We also provide a courtesy limousine to pick you up and take you to the marriage licence bureau.

You pay $35 for the marriage licence. There is no blood test and no waiting period required. The couple just fill out a form with their name, age and address and where they were born. It takes about ten minutes to get your licence.

We have flowers, photographs, videos, t-shirts, everything to make their wedding day the most beautiful day of their lives. And we are open 24 hours a day. We never close. There is a minister on duty the whole time. And we also have the world famous drive-up wedding window where you can get married in your car for $30. You just stay in your car and we marry you through the drive-up wedding window.

Then if you prefer you can be married in our beautiful garden gazebo and that also costs $30.

Oh, and there's the wedding chapel in the sky. The balloon is wonderful. It costs $125 per person. We go up about 2,000 feet over the city of Las Vegas. But first of all, the night before we take you down to get your marriage licence and then the next morning we pick you up about 5.30 and we marry you at the crack of dawn and you start your day over the city of Las Vegas. It takes about an hour, an hour and a half, and after your ceremony we find a place to land and climb out of the basket of the balloon and take you back to your hotel.

I'm known as the Wedding Queen of the West simply because I've been doing weddings for a long time, I've done over a half a million weddings in my life. Las Vegas is the marriage capital of the world and there's many different ways to get married here. There are people who come here who have wanted to get married on roller coasters, at the motor speedway, on horseback on mountain tops, in swimming pools. People want to get married in so many different ways. I try to provide weddings for people who want something unusual and different.

...we also have the world famous drive-up wedding window where you can get married in your car for $30.

CHARLOTTE RICHARDS

Oh, and there's the wedding chapel in the sky. The balloon is wonderful. It costs $125 per person. We go up about 2,000 feet over the city of Las Vegas.

CHARLOTTE RICHARDS

People take weddings very seriously here. I believe that the reason they come to Las Vegas to get married is it's very inexpensive and it's sort of like a holiday, a honeymoon and a wedding all wrapped into one package. I do think it's too easy to get married here sometimes. But I'd rather see them married then living together in sin.

I have married celebrities like Bruce Willis and Demi Moore. Their wedding was quite romantic, it was right at the strike of midnight and I only had about 15 minutes' notice. I can still see them now. They really love each other. Then there was Michael Jordan. What a wonderful person. What a great man. And Judy Garland, I will never forget her wedding. It was just absolutely breathtaking. It was beautiful. I couldn't help but cry, everything was so elegant. Everything was so simple but yet she was so beautiful. I remember Joan Collins. She laughed. She's just so joyous. And Mickey Rooney. What a wonderful, fun man he is. He recently sent me a Christmas card thanking

> *...I was ready to absolutely drop at the end of the 24-hour period, 224 weddings later.*
>
> CHARLOTTE RICHARDS

me because I'm going to be doing his children's weddings very soon.

Frank Sinatra got married in about 1967 at the Sands Hotel. I had to make arrangements for his flowers and his photography and the whole thing. He is a wonderful person and he's been part of many people's romantic life because of the songs that he sings.

The most weddings that I've done in a day was several years ago when Valentine's Day popped up on a Saturday. And of course Saturday is the busiest day of the week. But Valentine's Day is the busiest day of the year. And don't ask me how I did it because I can tell, I was ready to absolutely drop at the end of the 24-hour period, 224 weddings later.

The most number of marriages for one particular person? Oh, I don't even like to talk about him. He is absolutely disgusting. I think he's been married, like, 28 or 29 times. He does it for publicity and I don't find that interesting at all.

The other night two stars who are the main attraction in *Starlight Express* asked me to come and perform a wedding for them. And they dropped me down onto the main floor from a stage 20 feet up. And I walked out there among all the skaters and an audience of about 2,000 people and performed their wedding ceremony. It was beautiful. It was Las Vegas. It was the bright lights. This couple met in *Starlight Express*, he proposed to her on stage. Why not get married on stage? That's nothing uncommon. It's something beautiful.

Elvis - he was Mr Las Vegas. He was the King of Rock and Roll. He was a very sentimental, loving, caring person. His image will live on throughout eternity, because people found him romantic, singing all those beautiful love songs. We have Elvis impersonators that are invited to the chapel by various couples who get married here - they want him to walk them down the aisle and sing *Love Me Tender* to them. And that's what Las Vegas is all about - love.

"...that's what Las Vegas is all about - love.

CHARLOTTE RICHARDS

KATHLEEN, MINISTER:
Well, I own the Divine Madness Fantasy Wedding Chapel. You can come here and either get married in the traditional white gown and tuxedo or you can have a theme wedding. Your marriage can have a leather and chain motif, that's a very popular fantasy. In fact, it's so popular I'm thinking of decorating a chapel with leather walls, shackles and stuff. It's all an illusion, a fantasy.

I've done more Caesar and Cleopatra weddings than anything else. I think there's a lot to them. There's a lot of jewellry, a lot of gold. They're very dramatic outfits. Then there's Scarlet O'Hara and Rhett Butler, and there's the Renaissance weddings which are pretty popular. There's the Camelot look. Let's see, gangsters are pretty good. They love to do eras: '20s, '30s, '40s, '50s. A lot of '50s, the Elvis Presley time. And I've got a chrome jumpsuit effect on a space theme. All these outfits are dramatic and glamourous.

"I've done more Caesar and Cleopatra weddings than anything else. There's a lot of jewellry, a lot of gold."
KATHLEEN

SUSAN POWTER, FITNESS GURU:
Vegas? You know they have a roller coaster now on top of a hotel. I can't think of a place I dislike more than Las Vegas. To me, other than LA, Las Vegas is truly a city of broken dreams. Talk about whoring people! People come with all the money they've got, they come with their year's worth of savings and they go for that one chance. It is such a whore city. It makes my skin crawl.

But I would consider a Vegas wedding. I think that's pretty cool. You know, like an Elvis theme. If you're gonna do it, why not go totally trailer? You could have a stripper theme, a showgirl theme. Vegas, I don't judge it, I just don't go near it. Vegas gives me hives.

MULTIPLE MARRIAGES

LINDA ESSEX, 22-TIMES MARRIED:
I met some of my husbands in restaurants. Some I have just known all my life. One was a school friend. I met a lot of them in bars.

I am the world's most married woman. I'm now ready to get married again - it will be marriage number 23 and it's going to last forever. No more divorces and no more annulments. I think this one was meant to be. He's a sweet, kind person and I care a lot for him. I know that we are going to stay married. This is going to work.

I only wanted one marriage just like any other women. But it just didn't work out like that.

Scotty is 88 years old and he has been married 28 times and I will be wife number 29. We're both in the *Guinness Book of World Records*. Wc are both Leos and we've got a lot in common.

All my ex-husbands are friends with one another and I am friends with all of them.

JESSIE CHANDLER, ONE OF LINDA'S EXES:
I don't feel very good about it. But what can I do? She [Linda] has a mind of her own. I don't try and tell her what to do. Every time she gets married I feel bad.

I have been married to Linda twice. She's a perfect wife for any man. She's a good cook, a great woman, a great housekeeper and loves jewellry. You can't get better women. I still love Linda, I always will.

GLEN 'SCOTTY' WOOD, 28-TIMES MARRIED:
The youngest woman that I married was 14 years old. At the time I was 77. She was a perfect wife but she didn't know how to be good. She stayed with me for six years. I sent her to college and to high school. One day I found out that she was growing up. She wanted to take off somewhere so she just got her things and left.

> *Scotty is 88 years old and he has been married 28 times and I will be wife number 29.*
>
> LINDA ESSEX

Some people think that I am a dirty old man because I married them all. There have been several favourites, all with different ways. And some you like better then others. But they were all wonderful. They were young and trusting and they wanted to live right.

SUSAN POWTER:

Married 29 times? I would say that there is something a little off. I'd like to talk to this guy and ask him why. I'd like to know his reasons. What the hell is the matter with this guy? And what the hell is the matter with wife number 27 and 28? What are you going to say to your-self, 'Well, he's agreed to marry me. Yes, he's done it 28 times before, but this is really it, and I'm really going to change him this time.' Loser game!

KENNEDY, MTV PRESENTER:
29 times? That's a little excessive. I would get into a 12-step program.

STEPHANIE BEACHAM, ACTRESS:
Brilliant! 29 times! What optimism. How sweet. How dear. In California? In California with those laws? How many dining room tables has he given away?

> *Some people think that I am a dirty old man because I married them all. But they were all wonderful.*
> GLEN 'SCOTTY' WOOD

Well, she knows what she's going to be doing, doesn't she? She is going to nurse him for the rest of his life.

She must know what she's doing, I suppose. Is he very rich? No? Oh, poor girl! With a big age difference, more than ten years either way? I think it's a hard situation.

SORRELL TROPE, CELEBRITY LAWYER:
I would seriously suggest that this individual who is about to marry wife number 29 takes a very, very close look at himself in the mirror and asks, 'What is wrong that I have this need to be married, divorced, married, divorced that number of times?'

KELLY LANGE:
Do I think a chap who's been through 28 marriages is being reasonable about matrimony? Well, what can I say? If it works for him and if these women can stand it without killing him, I guess everybody's happy.

BIG AGE DIFFERENCES

DIANE CONWAY, COMEDIENNE AND FAIRY GODMOTHER:
The very best age gap is to be 12 years older than the man. My husband, my prince, is 12 years younger than me. In our consciousness, in our mind, in our heart and soul, we're all the same age anyway. It works perfectly. I waited and waited for a relationship. When I was a little girl in South Carolina I used to get down on my knees and say 'Now I lay me down to sleep, send a man, don't make him a creep.' (Or a cousin - that kind of thing happens in the south.)

KELLY LANGE:
The ideal age gap? I don't think there is one. Certainly not chronological age and, anyway, men are children. We love them. We can't live with them, we can't shoot them, but we love them.

Of course, it's an age-old cliche for an older man to marry a younger woman, like Anna Nicole Smith in her '20s, marrying that 90 year old man. It's all fun. I don't think chronological age is going to be the key to success. I think maturity is and who among us has that?

Susan Sarandon and Tim Robbins, isn't that wonderful? We're all jealous. We'd like to kill her. We think it's perfect. Goldie Hawn and and Kurt Russell, doing well. They're not married by the way, neither of those two couples, but it's working out nicely.

Marriage can be lethal. As soon as you put it down on paper, something else happens. I must admit that I'm fearful now for Melanie Griffith and Antonio Banderas who just got married.

But if a man starts getting old and cranky, then maybe he needs somebody who's older and crankier than he is to get along with him. Personally, I'm going to go look for a young stud now, I think I've had it with old men for a while.

DOE GENTRY, SINGLES CORRESPONDENT:
The older woman has already done the traditional things. She's been married and had children, either she's a career woman or she's had her career, she's invested, she's got her things, her toys. She doesn't need a man to buy for her, so younger men seem to be a really good match for a fun relationship, a friendship. And the younger men seem to know how to be friends. They are emotionally available to us. And women love that.

> *You cannot let your ego get in the way and think, 'Gee, I'm 65 years old and he's a 31 year old who really thinks I'm hot.*
> JOAN RIVERS

Younger men tell me they are looking for someone they can talk to, someone that has a mind, someone that can turn on their body and their mind. They tell me they are tired of being jerked around emotionally by younger women. They say that older women don't have as many expectations as far as the future is concerned, like children and that type of thing, because she's already done that. But I would advise older woman to be careful that the younger man doesn't want children because that can be heartbreaking if you start dating somebody and get into a serious relationship.

A lot of older women, women over 40, think that they're not that valuable because their looks are fading. But the younger man doesn't see that. He doesn't see the wrinkles, he's not looking at you for your wrinkles, he'd better not! I'll kill him, he knows better. It's not about that. It's about the inner beauty I think that they are capable of seeing and they're not intimidated. The younger man is not intimidated by a powerful woman because he has the inner resources to deal with it. He won't play these sexist games with your mind like some older men do.

Tina Turner has a younger man. There's Liz Taylor, but she doesn't anymore, that one didn't work out. Roseanne Barr. Cher, of course, she always has one. Mary Tyler Moore is married to a younger man.

DAVID CARRADINE, ACTOR:
I think I would find it difficult to spend all my waking hours with someone who hadn't graduated from high school yet.

> *If a 22-year-old toy boy came up to me, expressing his undying love, I would suspect his mental health.*
> PHYLLIS DILLER

PHYLLIS DILLER, COMEDIENNE:
If a 22-year-old toy boy came up to me, expressing his undying love and wanted to marry me, I would suspect his mental health, and then I would throw-up. But I do know an old writer who supported a young fella. They lived at the beach just sleeping around like crazy. How could he do that? She was so ugly. She had ugly teeth. She had a lot of wrinkles. She had never done anything to make herself look any better, but she was famous and rich so there he was jumping on her. Get a trampoline, sonny! Jump on something that will do you good.

When you see these old guys with these bimbos, these young airhead blondes, you know what is going on. The girl is doing it for money, she's his chattel, his showgirl, his show thing and it's kind of a joke. You can always tell a first wife. You can always tell a second.

KITTY FOX, PORN STAR:
I think older women and younger men just came out of the closet a couple of years ago. It is always been socially acceptable for older men and younger women. To see an older woman with a younger man used to be terrible.

The younger man knows that she is going to continue getting older and so is he, and that is what he likes. I think the best thing to do is to ask a younger man who is into older women what he thinks. They are not stupid, they know that she is not always going to be 50.

JOAN RIVERS, COMEDIENNE
You cannot let your ego get in the way and think, 'Gee, I'm 65 years old and he's a 31 year old who really thinks I'm hot. I mean, just get undressed and look in the mirror. Your breasts may be wonderful but your eyes are looking six inches below where they used to look.'

LEE METZENBAUM, MARRIED TO A YOUNGER WOMAN:
The age difference between us is 40 years exactly. Terri is 38 years old and I'm 78. And we can't change it, we can't make it any less, we have to accept what it is.

"Look at Anna Nicole Smith – she married that nice healthy man, a hundred years old, and she just rolled over and squished him!

RHONDA, SEX SYMBOL DYNASTY GROUP

TERRY METZENBAUM, LEE'S WIFE:
I feel the level of maturity of my husband is a great plus especially when I see some of the complications that arise with my friends whose husbands aren't as mature.

> *I would advise all my old friends to find themselves somebody younger, so they can experience the same pleasures in life.*
> LEE METZENBAUM

He has lived a great part of his life and had great experiences that he could bring into the marriage. Some might say that's not positive because we didn't do these things together, but I found them positive, because I don't need to learn from my mistakes because he's made a lot of mistakes.

I think that not having to deal with his middle-age crisis is another aspect. I have friends and their husbands are hitting 40 and 50, and not knowing what to do with the next 50 years of their lives. Well, he was past all that when I met him.

LEE METZENBAUM:
I feel young all the time, but it's a different existence when you're married to a person your own age. If I was married to a person of 75 I'm sure that we would have a different life. Particularly having a 12-year-old daughter, it's like having a whole brand new life.

I would advise all my old friends to find themselves somebody younger

TROPHY WIVES

KELLY LANGE:

The concept of the trophy wife intrigues me. It's a term that was coined by *Fortune* magazine seven years ago when they did an article about 15 or 20 prominent trophy wives of our day. They defined the trophy wife as the second, third, fourth or fifth wife of a very wealthy mogul who is usually a decade or two, or in the case of Anna Nicole Smith, seven decades, younger and who is made up meticulously from breakfast to lunch, through into the afternoon and cocktails and dinner and theatre and parties, who is dressed, stunningly, in couture, who is quaffed within an inch of her life and whose job it is to be a trophy, to be his prize, to be on his arm.

> *The trophy wife... is dressed in couture, is quaffed within an inch of her life and whose job it is to be a trophy – to be his prize, to be on his arm.*
>
> KELLY LANGE

Have I been a trophy wife? Yes of course.

Trophy wives aren't really just a Hollywood phenomenon. Trophy wives are everywhere. They're here, they're in Aspen, they're in New York, they're on the continent, they're everywhere. That's because of the way the phenomenon arises: a man spends years struggling to get his company going with his first wife. She is usually his age, she is the one who has the children, the one who wears the blue and white print dress with the white shoes 'cause she doesn't know any better, who's working hard, struggling along with him. And then he becomes successful and feels he deserves a trophy on his arm.

And when a man gives a dinner party for his colleagues, the first wife cooks, the trophy wife caters. The first wife shops at inexpensive places, the trophy wife has charge accounts everywhere: Barney's, Cartier, Tiffany, everywhere because by that time he's got loads of money.

Trophy wives are everywhere. When you see one, you'll think, 'Oh, look at him with her! Is that his daughter?' But of course it's not, it's his trophy wife!

OLIVIA GOLDSMITH, AUTHOR OF *FIRST WIVES CLUB*:
I think men are very silly if they think that they can get away with having someone twenty years younger. What do I always say? First wives want a stable home and trophy wives want a home with stables. Why would that enhance your self-esteem? I don't get it.

SHERRI SPILLANE, SCANDAL AGENT:
I was a trophy wife, I think it's terrific. I had a wonderful time. Mickey took me all over the world and it was fun and it was exciting. I think it's wonderful for the man and I think it's wonderful for women. It's not good for the ex-wife who gets left behind, I think that's terrible. I

> *Trophy wives are everywhere. When you see one, you'll think, 'Oh, look at him with her! Is that his daughter?, But of course, it's not, it's his trophy wife!*
>
> KELLY LANGE

have a lot of friends who were married to very famous men and most of them were left for younger women. I think that's very, very sad. Somebody has to get hurt, unfortunately. If there's no one getting hurt, I think it's fine, let them do what they want to do, let them have fun. Who says people have to be the same age? Everybody has different needs, as long as it's within the law, let them do it. It could be an older women with a younger man, that happens too. Great, terrific, just don't get hurt.

> *What do I always say? First wives want a stable home and trophy wives want a home with stables.*
> OLIVIA GOLDSMITH

DOUGLAS BAGBY, CELEBRITY LAWYER:
I understand the term trophy wife refers to those men who marry a woman because of her beauty and because she will look good attached to his arm while attending various events, parties and so forth. Such relationships can work for both people if it's clear to both of them that that is the basis of their relationship and that it may not be based on love or romance but upon both of their need to be perceived in a certain way. I'm not going to judge the basis upon which they decide to stay together.

DR RACHEL COPELAN,
COUPLES COUNSELLOR AND HYPNOTHERAPIST:
Trophy wives? Oh yes, there are trophy boys too. There are boy toys that are trophies. I noticed on the cover of the *Enquirer* that Liza Minnelli has this young man, a gorgeous 20 year old, and that's a trophy.

Trophy wives appear when men suddenly get a lot of money, and their wives are a little past the point of being teenage-looking, they've put on a little weight, or whatever, and the man starts thinking he's so great because he's got money.

STEPHANIE BEACHAM:
Men with trophy wives, they're idiots aren't they? 'Cause those girls are going to grow up. And by the time they're 35 their eyes aren't going to be as wide, they're just going to be on the make, once they've got the alimony, they'll dump him. It's the route to heartache.

LISA STAHL, ACTRESS, *BAYWATCH NIGHTS*:
I think a trophy wife in Los Angeles is very common. I see older gentlemen, usually very wealthy, very established, who have these women who are younger than their daughters that have all the plastic surgery head to toe. They're not always especially intelligent but they look good, they're an arm piece.

And it saddens me. I mean if they're really in love with each other fine, but I can't imagine that these women lust after these guys. You've got to be kidding me! Some of them look like turtles, they're all wrinkly. It's different when you're 70 and your man is 70. But I place as much blame on the women as I do on the men. It's absolutely preposterous.

BETTE MIDLER, ACTRESS:

I'm sure it happens everywhere, but only amongst a certain class. I think it's almost a function of ageing. I think men get anxious and they feel that they could go back if they had a younger, better-looking woman.

> *Wives usually remind them of what they are. They look at her and they see themselves and they don't want to see that.*
>
> BETTE MIDLER

SAME-SEX WEDDINGS

DAVE KULMAN, GAY MATCHMAKER:

I've been to many gay commitment ceremonies. Legally you can't actually get married but there are priests and ministers who perform these ceremonies and the couples get certificates.

ARLAN, WHO IS 'MARRYING' DAVID:

Some of my family will be there and friends that we've known in other parts of our lives, so it's going to be an interesting confluence of people that we've known in various capacities. And it will be kind of fun. We informally refer to it as a wedding, but, of course, there's no legal capacity to get married. I do wish that there could be. It would be wonderful!

The ceremony will be like a wedding. We've adapted it, but the adaptations are more for us personally than they are because we happen to be two men instead of a man and a woman. We've definitely stayed with a traditional type of Jewish ceremony which is fairly loose to begin with.

I think basically it will be the same relationship, but there'll be a deepness there because of the support of the community that we've felt so strongly. But, in many ways, it will go on the same.

I was married for 13 years, I think it was. So, I have two children, both of whom will be there, and my ex-wife will also be there. Then after my marriage ended I was in another relationship for three years that broke up a little over a year ago, and I had been out of that relationship for about two or three months when I met David. And that person I had that three year relationship with will also be there. He's excited about it.

It's kind of joyful for me. It's a way of putting together the different parts of my life. There are people coming who I met when I very first came out, when I was just divorced and was pretty much at the lowest part of my life.

> *We informally refer to it as a wedding, but, of course, there's no legal capacity to get married.*
>
> ARLAN

I know that Amy, my daughter, is excited about it. She's going to be escorting me up the aisle. Amy is 16 and my son, Adrian, is 12 and he'll be here too. I don't think he's quite as excited about it. But he and I have never been quite as close anyway, it's just a personality thing. But I think he'll be glad that he's here and participating. He doesn't have to say anything, he didn't want to, so Amy's going to say all the words. But he will be one of the ring bearers. And we invited his mother and he was unwilling to come without her, and she encouraged him to come. I wasn't sure how she would feel about it but she called up and left a really nice message. And, my mom will be riding to the ceremony with her, so it will work out really well.

I think we basically decided to do this ceremony because we thought of it as an ideal opportunity for joy in the community. The gay community is one that's been decimated by a great deal of sorrow and a lot of tragedy and there's not as much opportunity for joy as we would like. So we wanted this so we could share our joy with the whole community and so that we could say to them, 'Let's remember to celebrate the things that are there to be celebrated.'

LISA, RABBI FOR DAVID AND ARLAN:
In the last ten years there's been a growth in same-sex marriages and especially in the last five. You can tell by going to any bookstore and looking in the wedding-book section and seeing how many books there are now just for planning gay and lesbian weddings. There's a real market for it.

> *We basically decided to do this ceremony because we thought of it as an ideal opportunity for joy in the community.*
> ARLAN

In the Los Angeles community, I have yet to see any hotel, or even synagogue for that matter, bat an eye about having a gay or lesbian ceremony on their facility. That's partly for economic reasons, I'm sure, and it's partly just Los Angeles, but I think it says something about the amount of them we have now and a kind of the acceptance that's grown, at least in our city.

AMY, ARLAN'S DAUGHTER:
I am just so happy for them, you know. They found each other, and I wish it could be like that for me. I'm like, 'Wow!'

When I found out that my dad was gay I thought it was probably for the best. That's what's really helped me get through it, whereas my brother and my mom are still sad about it. But I thought it was good and then I came out myself. And it made it easier for me. I was sad at first, then I was kind of happy, I don't know. It's kind of a mixed feeling.

SUCCESSFUL RELATIONSHIPS

DIANE CONWAY:

This is a disposable society, more than anywhere else in the world. It's get a new car, get a new dress, get a new face, throw it away if it doesn't work. So, people don't understand that they need to let things develop.

People need to work at a marriage to keep it romantic and keep it alive. The most important thing you need to do is respect the other person, to have a really deep respect for that person, to honour that person, to know that they are not going to be at the top of their form all the time, to know that they're a unique human being and to accept them.

DENISE GILBERT, MISS FLIRT USA:

The important things are honesty and communication. Acceptance of who the other person is. And knowing that a relationship is growing all the time.

ANDY, GUEST AT SINGLES PARTY:

Unfortunately, people choose with their hormones rather than with their brains. They choose somebody who turns them on visually but with whom they are incompatible. You've heard the expression that opposites attract and they do. Unfortunately, opposites don't stay together, eventually they move apart. Once the excitement is gone, they find that they really can't live with each other. So the most important thing is choose somebody like you. Somebody who shares your values. Somebody on a similar intellectual level, with a similar belief system.

SORRELL TROPE:

The key to a successful marriage is having an ability to like your spouse.

KELLY LANGE:

In my opinion, the key to a successful marriage in Hollywood is separate houses. In my last marriage, we had separate houses. It worked wonderfully until we moved in together. It worked well when we lived next door to each other for some time. He would pick me up for a date to go to dinner. That was lovely. People talk about having separate rooms, but separate houses are better or separate cities. I have a friend who's a writer and she and her husband live in separate counties. He lives down in Orange County and she lives in LA. Living on separate coasts is good, like New York and LA - those bi-coastal marriages work well. But the best of all possible worlds would be separate countries.

There are some wonderful Hollywood marriages. I think perhaps it might be a generational thing. Jimmy Stewart was married to his wife for a long, long time. I know Gregory Peck and Veronique, they've been married for a long time. He's just turned eighty and they have a wonderful life. They spend half of it in France and half of it in America. There are lots of good, long term marriages, but it seems to be among the older generation. I don't know of any among today's generation.

> *❝ the key to a successful marriage in Hollywood is separate houses. But the best of all worlds would be separate countries.❞*
> KELLY LANGE

SHERRI SPILLANE AND RUTH WEBB, SCANDAL AGENTS:
Sherri: For a successful relationship you need sex, a lot of sex. A lot of money, a lot of romance, a lot of excitement. How can you go wrong?

Ruth: How did you?

Sherri: Very easily, it was a joke. I think I have bad taste in men. I look for the exciting men and the exciting men are always trouble.

DOUGLAS BAGBY:

There's a lot of speculation as to why the divorce rates are no longer increasing. Some people are suggesting that it may have to do with HIV, others think it may have something to do with economics. People spend more money apart than they do if they consolidate the resources and stay together. Maybe it has something to do with sophistication. Maybe people are staying together because mental health professionals have contributed to our education in terms of understanding ourselves and others.

GEORGE FALARDEAU, PLAYBOY:

I can say without a doubt that the American nuclear family as we once knew it in the '50s is disappearing, if not gone all together. It's partly because you are getting two people working within one household. But I still think that a balance can be achieved between a working husband and a working wife. The attention given to children today is not there. The American family as we once knew it is gone.

ROGER CLINTON, BROTHER OF BILL:

Celebrity marriages are going to have a tougher time from the outset. Much more so than regular marriages, because of the media. You have to deal with it. I think that a lot of celebrities live in a fantasy world. I think

> *Celebrity marriages are going to have a tougher time from the outset. I think a lot of celebrities live in a fantasy world.*
> ROGER CLINTON

sometimes they're not as realistic as they need to be. They think that they can separate their lives, keep their business celebrity lives completely separate from their personal lives and maintain their privacy. And it just can't be done. I think the successful ones probably realize that the media ís going to play a big part.

DOYLE BARNETT, COUPLES MEDIATOR:
I did a survey a little over six years ago, of couples who had been married for over 50 years, and the number one issue that they said kept them together was trust.

PHYLLIS DILLER:
How to treat a husband is very simple - treat him like a dog. When he comes home at night, say to him what you say to the dog, 'Oh, itsy bitsy pooh poo, oh let me scratch your ears'. And meet him at the door with his slippers, and then sit him down and give him a Martini and pet him a little. Treat him like a dog. Don't greet him at the door saying, 'The washing machine broke again, see if you can fix it this time, you idiot'.

Don't hit him with everything that went wrong in your day. He's tired, he's had a bad day.

KENNEDY:
The key to a successful relationship is friendship. You have to be friends. Because you'd never screw one of your friends over.

GOLDIE HAWN:
I don't believe in marriage, I don't believe in the whole process. The lawyers, the rules, whether it's in a church

> *How to treat a husband is very simple: treat him like a dog. When he comes home at night, say to him what you say to the dog.*
>
> PHYLLIS DILLER

167

> *"Take it with a bit of humour. None of it is easy, none of life is easy, not one bit of it. And you have to be able to roll with the punches.*

BETTE MIDLER

or a synagogue. Nothing matters. What matters is how you live each day. One ceremony to proclaim your love for each other can be annihilated in three years. It doesn't mean anything. If it did, then I would say it is important, but you can't legislate love.

I think that we have maintained our individuality. I think that I have a great amount of respect for his brain. I respect him as a human being. He respects me. We have the same values where growing up is concerned. We've raised our children with pretty much the same idea of what's right and wrong. We play really well together. We're great playmates. I can go away by myself. I have a life of my own and he has a life of his own, and it makes it more romantic when you get together.

BETTE MIDLER:
Take it with a little bit of humour. None of it's easy, none of life is easy, not one bit of it. And you have to be able to roll with the punches, be flexible and not get bogged down in the small stuff.

I do believe in marriage, I absolutely believe in marriage. I believe in marriage for the sake of the children. But marriage is a tough road to hell. I don't recommend it for anyone who isn't going to have children, I really don't, unless they are completely committed to the idea, unless they have a fire that they have to do this. Because people who don't have a fire are not going to work at it.

This word relationship is a new word, it's less than 100 years old. People didn't used to have relationships. People used to have partnerships, you know, or people had arranged marriages and you brought all your possessions together and you were suddenly wealthier, twice as wealthy as you used to be. And then the guy was responsible for bringing home the food and the woman was responsible for the home. But this is all relatively new, all this relationship stuff. And nobody really knows what it is. And they don't stop dissecting this crap for a second. They write about it in books, they write about it in magazines, they're constantly talking about it, 'My relationship, my relationship!'

I mean, you just want to die. You want to say, 'Sod your relationship, go read a book or something'. These people, they don't have anything to do but talk about this crap. Don't talk about it, live it.

STEPHANIE BEACHAM:

The key to a successful relationship? Somebody once told me that their definition of the best sex was with 'someone whose name I never quite got, who's going to Australia tomorrow'. I think expectation is the thing that kills relationships. Take what you're given. That is your relationship. Don't expect more. Don't dream. Then you see what's really on the table and what you can do with it.

DENNIS FRANZ:

The key to a successful relationship is, respect for one another. You can't be selfish all the time and you have to understand what the other person needs. It's a continuous compromise. And a very worthwhile one.

GENA LEE NOLIN:

I think the most important thing is communication. I mean that certainly is what is keeping my marriage together. It's very hard but communication is number one, along with a mutual respect for one another.

Hollywood's most successful romantic relationship? I would think that would be Demi Moore and Bruce Willis. One, because they've lasted now for about eight years which is hard to do and they have three children and they really take part in rearing them and instilling decent priorities in them. I think the public respect that and that's one of the reasons they're both so admired.

JAY LENO, CHAT SHOW HOST:

Just try not to find the key. I enjoy women but I don't want to be a gynaecologist. Keep the mystery.

> *Just try not to find the key. I enjoy women, but I don't want to be a gynaecologist. Keep the mystery.*
>
> JAY LENO,
> CHAT SHOW HOST

CHAPTER FOUR

Broken Dreams in Hollywood

> " Take it with a little bit of humour. None of life's easy, not one bit of it.
>
> BETTE MIDLER "

INTRODUCTION

And so to life after marriage, the broken dreams, the disappointments and as statistics show, divorce. In a society where love is dispensed with for the chance of younger love, wealthier love, the penalty is high. Literally high for those who have to cough up for settlements that soar into millions of dollars.

If you've been accustomed to flying only in a private plane, why should that have to change simply because your husband left you for a floozie? Women argue that they have become used to a lifestyle that costs $50,000 a month to maintain. It gets messy and bloody and the acrimony can be fierce. 'Is Hollywood bad for wife-dumping?' ponders Olivia Goldsmith, 'Hollywood invented wife-dumping!' And if you've been dumped, there's only one thing to do, says Diane Conway, 'Just wallow in it.' Then get out there and, 'get a new one'.

Private investigators sift through the contents of trash cans for evidence of infidelity, divorce lawyers thrash out the details and mediators do their best to calm everything down.

Pre-nuptial agreements are drawn up in an attempt to protect couples from too much acrimony should the marriage fail. Bette Midler says, 'Don't get married without one!' but Stephanie Beacham lends a cautionary voice and believes it is sad when, 'Your love is tempered by the sort of reality that says, "But just in case, honey"'. Many are worried by the state of marriage in Los Angeles. They believe that expectations are too high, that in a city where so much is disposable, marriage too is seen as throw-away. If it's not working, don't fix it, just throw it away and get another one.

Christine O'Keefe, a Beverly Hills matchmaker, says, 'Unless we repair the American family that we once held as such a treasure, I'm afraid this country is doomed for a lot more disaster than it's ready to deal with.'

> *This is a tragic place. People are in and out of celebrity, they're in and out of movies and they're in and out of marriage.*
>
> KELLY LANGE,
> AUTHOR

Unhappy Relationships

Debra Winkler, president, Personal Search Dating Agency:

I read the other day that the statistic for divorce in Southern California is as much as 60 per cent of all marriages. Isn't that shocking?

Everybody thinks that Prince Charming will come along on a white horse or the princess will come along and they'll live happily ever after.

Patti, member, Club 40-Something Dating Group:

I was married for 15 years and it didn't work out. He liked to screw around. He hit 40 and mid-life crisis set in and every woman he saw, he wanted. And I couldn't deal with that.

Divorce is very painful to go through. That's why it amazes me that so many people today are getting divorced. I think too many people go into marriage thinking, 'Well, if it doesn't work out, we'll get divorced'. And to me that's the craziest, craziest thing to hear because divorce is so painful.

Diane Conway, comedienne and Fairy Godmother:

The first thing you do when you have a broken heart is you got to wallow in it. Just wallow in it. It is going to hurt for a while and you've just got to get used to it. So put on your old bathrobe with the coffee stains down the front, put on the TV or, better yet, play real sad Country music, you know, some tear-jerker stuff. Get yourself some decadent chocolates, stuff yourself. Call all your friends and tell them it's the end of the world and cry. Then get up the next day, take a shower, do your hair, go out and buy new make-up, and say to yourself, 'I may be down, but I'm not out' and get out there and get a new one. There's a new one comes by every 20 minutes, just like a bus.

> *If you're seeking revenge, you'll never get over it. I think that the best thing is living well, letting go, going on.*
>
> DIANE KEATON,
> ACTRESS

I always say there may be 50 ways to leave your lover, but all you need is one. And my three step program for getting over a bad relationship is: Stop It Now. And I'll be glad to come right over to your house and do that for you the next time you're with a nitwit or somebody who's not treating you right.

DENISE GILBERT, MISS FLIRT USA:
My girlfriend gave me a card and it hits the nail on the head. It says, 'Never cry over a man. Just yell "next!"'

SORRELL TROPE, CELEBRITY LAWYER:
I had a client who was married in the afternoon and by the early evening had decided that he didn't want to be married and came to me to try and obtain an annulment. That's the shortest marriage I know, a couple of hours.

OLIVIA GOLDSMITH, AUTHOR OF *FIRST WIVES CLUB*:
If you just take a look at Hollywood, it seems that one of the reasons marriages break up is because expectations are out of line with reality. Everyone's disappointed with themselves. I wake up every morning and I'm disappointed with myself 'cause I'm not still young and I'm not still pretty and why don't I look like Julia Roberts?

Is Hollywood bad for wife dumping? Hollywood invented wife-dumping.

I have a close friend, a guy, who after his relationship broke up and the woman cheated on him, he went out and spent tens of thousands of dollars on computer equipment that he didn't need, didn't use, didn't want. But, you know, it moved the pain around.

> *The best way to mend a broken heart for a woman is another man.*
> *What could be better?*
>
> KELLY LANGE, AUTHOR

SHERRI SPILLANE, SCANDAL AGENT:
Fix it as fast as you possibly can, anyway you can. It doesn't do any good to sit home and cry. There is a certain amoung of time that has to go by before you can pull up your boot straps and get with it. But just try to get with it as quickly as possible. Get your friends around you, go out, have a good time. Drink champagne, go out on the town. Life is short, why spend it moping?

DOE GENTRY, SINGLES CORRESPONDENT:
Men come to parties and their hearts are just bleeding. I think it hits men harder than it does women because women have the ability to go, 'That dirty, rotten so and so' to each other but guys just sit there and suffer silently. It's like impotency, they sit there and the world doesn't know and they don't get it out. I usually tell men that they've got to get out there and start dating again, you

> *One of the reasons that marriages break up is because expectations are out of line with reality. Everyone's disappointed.*
>
> OLIVIA GOLDSMITH

know, don't lose your relationship skills, don't lose the ability to bond. Just remember the good parts. But obsession can be a real problem for a lot of people. They just can't stop thinking about the other person.

DAVID CARRADINE, ACTOR:
My relationship failed and it was my fault. I just did not treat her well enough and I was unfaithful to her several times, mostly little one-night things, but then I finally had a really serious affair and that broke the thing open.

She was very young. She didn't really know what kind of a woman she was growing into. I was quite a bit older than her, but I was just as unfinished as she was.

I've been married three times, with the ceremony and the piece of paper. Barbara Hershey and I never married, but we were together for almost seven years and we have a full-grown son between us, so I don't see why I shouldn't say that I have been married four times.

So many divorces are the product of people giving up too easily because they do not accept the fact that life is difficult. They expect it to just be much easier. So when they hit a rocky road, instead of sticking in there and riding through it, they give up and bail out.

DIANE KEATON:
No, I don't think revenge works. I think that's the thing you absolutely must not do because it traps you eternally. If you're seeking revenge, you'll never get over it. I think that the best thing is living well, letting go, going on. Otherwise you're trapped, you're ruined, finished. It's over, goodbye, history, the end. I mean that's the worst.

> *So many divorces are the product of people giving up too easily because they do not accept that life is difficult.*
>
> DAVID CARRADINE

CHRISTINE O'KEEFE, MATCHMAKER:

I'm in my '40s and when I grew up, moms and dads got along. Parents didn't get divorced that often. If you had a neighbour on the block who was getting a divorce, that was big news. People worked out their problems. Now you have a lot of couples who are divorced and a lot of children being raised in single parent homes. They're not happy. They're angry. No one is dealing with their issues. If you grew up with a mom and dad who were unwilling to work out their problems and they divorced and then went off and married or lived with or dated other people, what concept do you have of marriage? Is it something that you work out or is it something that if it isn't working, you just abandon? Too many people abandon their marriages too easily.

Unless we repair the American family that we once held as such a treasure, I'm afraid this country is heading towards a lot more disaster than it's ready to deal with.

The reason I think there's a high failure rate in marriage in Hollywood is due to the nature of the beast. You're in an atmosphere where there's so much temptation. For both men and women.

If you're a working woman and you're successful, there are probably lots of other men interested in dating you. There are different standards here, I've learned. I'm from the Midwest and there if someone was married that was very much respected. In this town if someone's married, people don't seem to mind. Having an affair doesn't seem to carry a lot of weight.

There are a lot of people in the film community that have double standards and in a sense lead a double life. A lot of them are very bored. They've been given so much, they have so much opulence. They have these incredible homes, they have maids who do everything for them, they have servants galore. They have drivers, they have valets, they have a manicurist and a hairdresser, they have someone that dresses them, they have everything. But somewhere in the midst of all these

> *There are different standards here. Having an affair doesn't seem to carry a lot of weight.*
>
> CHRISTINE O'KEEFE

material things they have lost their sense of value. And so, they take it all very much for granted. Therefore, do they take marriage that seriously? No. It's like, 'This will be nice now, but you know, it's not forever, and if this doesn't work, well there'll be ten more people out there I could marry.' That seems to be a general attitude.

I'm not advocating that anybody stay in a relationship where they're in danger, or where they could die. I'm saying that if people are having arguments over money or religion or politics, or where the kids go to school, or who cuts the front lawn, or how you decorate the living room, get some help. Sit down and work out your issues. Go back to the basics. How did you meet? How did you fall in love? What made you fall in love? What did you like about each other? And go back and try to figure out if that's still there. Recreate it.

> *The reason there's a high failure rate in marriage in Hollywood is due to the nature of the beast.*
> CHRISTINE O'KEEFE

Some people come here wearing their emotions on their sleeve. They're very upset. A man came to me a little while ago who was so heartsick over this woman who had ended a relationship with him. She went back

to her husband, but she kept on calling him, she wanted to sort of keep him alive in the background, but she wanted to get on with her life with her husband.

She wasn't being fair. She made her choice, she went back to her husband. Well, this man was single, he was divorced with a daughter and he was so devastated by this woman that he was hardly able to get on with his day. So I made a deal with him. I said every time she calls you, or every time you're tempted to call her, I want you to go in the kitchen and open the freezer section of the refrigerator, and I want you to put one of your hands in there, on the ice cubes until you can't think anymore, until it hurts, and then call me.

Well, after many trips to the freezer and many phone calls, he associates those phone calls with pain. He associates physical pain with being in touch with her. Now he's able to detach himself from her.

Some people just have a very difficult time getting over a broken heart. Other people mend a little quicker.

Many people go from the frying pan into the frying pan. As soon as they're out of one relationship, they're in another one. They take no time in between to heal. They take no time to get in touch with who they are, to ask themselves, 'Why didn't that relationship work?' And, 'If this person did not deserve my trust, why was I with him or her? Why do I keep choosing that kind of person?' The people who ask themselves these questions are the types of people that do well with me because I'm able to break their patterns.

One of the classic statements I've heard from clients over the years is, 'Well, you know, I had a great time and this is a wonderful person, but they're not my type.' My response to that is, 'Great! Your type doesn't work and it never has. Your type can't give you trust, self-confidence, or a healthy relationship. So, kill your type. That isn't really your type, it's just what you perceive it to be. It's what's familiar and it's what's comfortable. But it's just not working for you.'

You're in an atmosphere where there's so much temptation. For both men and women.

CHRISTINE O'KEEFE

Living as a mistress was a lot of fun...

BRIDGET

BRIDGET, ESCORT:

I think this is a very difficult city to have a relationship in. Most of the men here seem to want multiple partners. I don't see too many couples who practise monogamy. There are a lot of drugs, a lot of drinking, a lot of partying. It's not exactly a lifestyle that's conducive to having a husband, a wife and a family. Also, people are very involved in their careers and their own lives. Within my own circle of friends, I notice a lack of commitment.

I think a lot of it has to do with the transient state of things in Los Angeles. People move here, and then they move away. There aren't too many people who have been born and raised here. Also, I think it's just a place people come to to have fun. They come to party, to get laid, and fool around.

They're bored with their wives, they want to feel younger so they go out with younger women. A lot of the time the wives are busy doing other things: they're busy with their children, busy with charities, busy with dogs, busy with God knows what, busy travelling and the men are sort of left on their own and they wander.

I think that if wives paid more attention to their husbands and simply spent more time with them and talked to them and got to know their husbands as people that there would be less cheating.

Living as a mistress was a lot of fun and I never really felt like a mistress because the person who I was with for many, many years always made me feel like a wife.

I was given all of the things that a husband would normally give a wife: a beautiful home, security, credit cards, ample money to do with whatever I wanted. In fact, I believe that I was given a lot more freedom than his wife. I don't know her but, from what I hear, her life was more controlled than mine was. I was able to travel, go to school, finish my education and, best of all, have a beautiful baby who is the most important thing in my life.

When I met him, he told me he was married and he told me that his wife and he had become estranged over the last several years and they were living separate lives and she was very involved with her doggies.

He hadn't been with anyone in a long time, least of all his wife and I think he just wanted to make sure that he still had it in him, and he did. And, we had a blast, and we still do and we've been together now for seven years.

He offered to take care of all my expenses and just began doing so.

I had a nice apartment in Paris and he wired me money for my expenses. In the beginning, he really didn't give me a lot because I didn't really need a lot: I was a student, I was studying. He was always very generous. He would come and take me on little trips to London and New York, we would go shopping and he would buy me whatever I wanted: fur coats, clothing, jewellry, we'd go to the theatre, to nice restaurants. When I came back and decided to go back to USC, which is where I was attending school, he set up an allowance and he gave me a specified amount and continued to pay my rent. And then, he made the mistake of giving me an American Express credit card which I maybe used to use a bit too much. There probably was a limit on it, but I never really found out what that was. In a bad month I could go through $50,000.

I lived in Paris for almost a year. I went with two suitcases and came back with 15. My little beach bungalow just wouldn't hold it all. So he bought me a Mercedes convertible and he said, 'You can't keep this Mercedes here at the beach, it will be stolen' and though I really liked my little beach place I was also thinking about where was I going to put all my new things. Where would I put all my new Vuitton luggage?

So, I found a house very close to where he was living. It was a large Victorian mansion in Malibu and actually on the same block as his house. Well, then the house was just all empty and 15 suitcases wasn't really enough to fill it up, so I started decorating and buying furniture. And I lived there for three years.

> *He offered to take care of all my expenses and just began doing so. In a bad month, I could go through $50,000.*
>
> **BRIDGET**

I used to drive by their house all the time and I used to always wonder if she was home, what they were doing. It was very odd, actually. One Christmas, I drove by their house and it was all lit up, the whole estate: the trees, the gates, the fences, the house, the windows, the doors and she was throwing a big, lavish party. I became incredibly jealous and went leaping through the yellow pages and called an electrician and had my house lit up too. Well, I had 70 windows so it turned out to be a rather expensive fit of jealousy. I think it cost almost $10,000.

And then she found out about me. He was having disagreements with his attorney, they were not getting along and the attorney, for whatever reason, told the wife about me and about our child. And, as the old saying goes, the shit hit the fan. Of course, she became very upset. She would call my house at all hours of the night wanting to talk about it. I talked to her several times and then I was advised by attorneys and my family not to talk to her anymore. So, I don't. Since then she has sued him for divorce and God willing, it will end quickly and we can be a family and get married and put this behind us.

> *Most of the men here seem to want multiple partners. I don't see too many couples who practise monogamy.*
> BRIDGET

EMILY SCOTT-LOWE, MARRIAGE THERAPIST:
How do you mend broken hearts? That's very difficult to answer because I've run into some hearts that just don't seem to be mendable. I wish I had the answer, then I'd bottle it and sell it and be a millionaire.

DR PAT ALLEN, RELATIONSHIP THERAPIST:
I could lock up and put in hospital more men with broken hearts than women. A man will kill himself four times faster than any woman if he believes he's with a

good and virtuous woman, and she's really a floundering, predatory, nymphomaniac.

Men are very sensitive creatures. Women, there's nothing as tough as a woman. And a man who still wants to be seen as a man, who puts his hope and his faith in a woman, and finds out that he's been betrayed, this person easily can lose his life, his career and his health. Whereas a woman who is strong inside is like a rock, and that woman can usually step over that and move on.

Dr Rachel Copeland,
couple's counsellor and hypnotherapist:
There are many couples who stay together. Goldie Hawn and Kurt Russell, for example. They're not even married and they have several children together, and she told me, 'We're doing fine just the way we are, and we ask the children, "Would you feel better if we got married?" And the children say, "No, it's fine"'. So some loving relationships do last in Hollywood.

Celebrities have more problems than any other group of people. More drugs, more alcohol, more smoking. I have a celebrity client who smokes five packs of cigarettes a day. You know, she makes millions for a movie, but she

smokes five packs, so what good are the millions going to do her?

DR PAT ALLEN:
Advice for broken hearts? Stay alive. Don't drink, don't use drugs, and duty date. Do you know what duty dating is? It's when you go out on a date and you would rather they drown in the chicken soup. Duty dating is when you watch the clock, when you can't stand being there. It's a horrible experience. I recommend it. You have to duty date, in order to stop eating pralines and cream and blowing up and committing suicide.

RHONDA AND JULIE, SEX SYMBOL DYNASTY GROUP:
You have to work at marriage. But here it's not like working at it like you do in Iowa. Here you have to stay looking like an 18 year old, you have to get every place lifted. You have to look good for the rest of your life. And that is a lot of pressure for a woman.

Julie: It's like putting yourself in a blender: you'd better be a damn good swimmer or you are going to get sucked down to the bottom and chopped into bits.

Rhonda: How do you mend a broken heart? I think retail therapy really works for me. Shopping is really good. That mends it for me. In fact, when you are in a store you never know who you are going to meet with a charge card.

> "*It's like putting yourself in a blender: you'd better be a damned good swimmer or you are going to get sucked down to the bottom and chopped into bits.*"
>
> JULIE

SHIRLEY LaSPINA,
WHO RUNS A GROUP FOR DIVORCED WOMEN:
The very first thing that I do to help women cope with the break up of a relationship is to get them to write their feelings down. Women have a tendency, I have found, to go over every single thing in their mind, from the minute they met the guy to when they broke up. They think, 'Why is this? How is that?' There are actually five or six stages that they've identified that you're gonna go through. You're gonna feel overwhelmed. You're gonna feel hurt. You're gonna feel angry. You're gonna want to kill him. And I say some of that stuff is really good.

SUSAN POWTER, FITNESS GURU:
Do I believe in marriage? I am astoundingly monogamous. But I don't really know 'cause I don't understand what it means. I haven't figured that out yet. I believe in commitment. Whether it's to raising my children or in my female relationships or in my business.

But I don't really see the point of marriage. If I did you better believe I'd have a pre-nuptial agreement signed, a post-nuptial agreement signed, a during-nuptial agreement signed. I would cover my bases on many levels. But I don't see the point. What's the point? Do I believe in being with somebody and committing to that and getting to a different level? Absolutely.

The best antidote for despair is action, as in, get on with your life. As in, hurt but don't collapse. As in, nothing should be so important that it takes over your being. Get over all the sappy stuff and get on with why you're hurting, and what you can do to avoid it later. I've been there. Absolutely, I've been there. And what I found is that no matter who's around me, I'm always left with me. So, things hurt and they get dented, and sometimes you have to take a step back, and sometimes you can't breathe for a couple of days but it shouldn't destroy you. If it does, it's a much bigger issue than the man who's just left.

I got married to John [Taylor] when I was 19… I was very young.

AMANDA DE CADANET

AMANDA DE CADANET:

My views on marriage? Well, I keep telling my daughter it's not like *Sleeping Beauty* and *Cinderella* and all those fairy stories.

I think marriage is the ultimate expression of your love for somebody. I mean, I love my husband hugely, immensely. I got married to John [Taylor] when I was 19 years old and I'm really happy that I made that choice. I was young, you know, I was very young. We don't live together but he's still my husband, I'm his wife. And I'm really happy that I'm married to John and we still go out to places and he'll say, 'This is my wife.' I think marriage is a wonderful thing, but most of them don't last. I consider my marriage as lasting.

If you marry out of desire and passion and lust and obsession, you've had it, it's just a matter of time. Because all that stuff wears off. If you marry someone because that person is an amazing companion and you have the most incredible, loving, caring friendship, whether you separate or whatever, you're always going to have that. I would probably get married again. I do feel it's important for a child to have parents that are married. But I don't know why I have this concept and it's completely at odds with everything else that I think.

Did my parents' divorce affect me? Yes it did, in a negative way, and I'm very careful not to repeating any of those elements with my child. And so far I think we've succeeded.

STEPHANIE BEACHAM:

Marriage, its easy to do, isn't it? Hell, I think it's probably harder to get a dog license in Hollywood than it is to get a marriage license. But divorce, oh dear, what a subject. They are hard to get, hard to agree on. All of the details. All of the vengeance. All the sadness, all the tears. The lawyers' fees.

Of course, you can calm yourself with pre-nuptials here, people do that the whole time. There are some extraordinary agreements. There are women running to their lawyers because their boyfriends might sue them for loss of standard of living. That's ridiculous, isn't it? That's without pride. I mean, 'I want my bicycle back' is fair enough, but 'My standard of living is going to be low because I'm no longer living off you'? Go out and get a job. Get a life.

I've only had one marriage. Oh dear, to delve that far into the past seems just about as boring as telling you about vomiting after being drunk for the first time. It just doesn't seem very relevant to my life now. I think people expect an awful lot and don't see what's really there. It's Walt Disney's fault, isn't it? 'One day my prince will come.' Daft! One day someone will come along with whom you may be able to forge a decent relationship if you both work hard enough at it.

The best way to mend a broken heart is exercise. Just get out and do it. Don't run into the arms of somebody else. Get out and get in the fresh air and play tennis and roller-blade and roller-skate and swim and laugh a lot. Definitely don't run into another relationship. But that's just so obvious, isn't it?

LISA STAHL, ACTRESS, *BAYWATCH NIGHTS*:
I definitely got married too young. I was 23 and I think at that age a lot of girls go through a stage where they have this idealistic image of marriage, they think of it as the wedding, the dress, the food, the party, but it's the part after that's so difficult.

He was very much into motorcycles and dirt and I loved glitter gowns and the Oscars. There was conflict. I think that marriages have a pretty tough time of it in Hollywood because there are so many beautiful people and humans are weak. If you have a box of chocolates - to quote Forrest Gump - how can you decide which one to pick? They're all so sweet and lovely looking. And also when you're on the set of a movie or a TV show for three, four or five months, it's very tempting.

He was very much into motorcycles and dirt and I loved glitter gowns and the Oscars.

LISA STAHL

STEPHANIE BEACHAM:
I think there's far too much choice, there's too much on offer here.

GENA LEE NOLIN, ACTRESS, *BAYWATCH*:
Mending a broken heart? Well, go home, take a hot bath, have lots of ice cream, and just remember that there are so many fish in the sea, that life is just beginning.

GOLDIE HAWN:
A broken heart takes time to mend so I think the first thing you have to do is acknowledge that it's okay to have a broken heart, that it happens to everyone. And then I think that you have to stop being the victim, recognize your pain and work through it physically, with physical exercise, by making sure you get out and be with your friends, going places and having fun, listening to music and reading lots of books about people who are wiser than we are, about how life does go on.

BETTE MIDLER:
What is the cure for a broken heart? Time and er... time. That's all. No amount of food will do it. I know because a lot of people try. Sometimes a new wardrobe will help, but really the answer is time.

> *What is the cure for a broken heart? No amount of food will do it.*
>
> BETTE MIDLER

INFIDELITY

DIANE CONWAY:
There's an awful lot of infidelity, perhaps you've noticed, and it's not a good idea for several reasons: it hurts people, it's very destructive. I don't want to sound real moral here, because I've done my things that I'm not too proud of, but I think it's better to be faithful. But of course it's hard.

Should women forgive men? Should men forgive women for committing adultery? It depends on the circumstances. Women are just as susceptible as men. If I were unfaithful I'd probably want to be forgiven. I'd like all the forgiveness I can get. That's another reason it's so hard for celebrities because if they have an indiscretion, everybody knows about it. Can you imagine how embarrassing that would be, to see something in the tabloids at the supermarket about your husband or wife fooling around? How embarrassing!

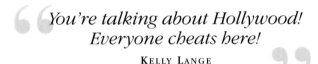

You're talking about Hollywood!
Everyone cheats here!

KELLY LANGE

SHERRI SPILLANE:
I think the older generation probably was a much safer generation for not fooling around and straying. When I think of the younger people, I think it's rampant today, I really do. And I think they're crazy because of AIDS. That would certainly stop me from doing what I used to do. I'd be very, very careful with any men that I got involved with now. I'd make them give me an AIDS test in writing, I'd want to talk to their doctor, I'd want to know the names of everybody they went with before.

RITA RUDNER, COMEDIENNE
Monogamy does exist in Hollywood, but I think it would be a lot more popular if it didn't sound so much like monotomy.

IAN, PARTNER OF ALEXANDRA PAUL,
ACTRESS, *BAYWATCH*
We have this discussion periodically about whether humans as a species are really designed to be monogamous or if there has been some outside influence that has lead us to believe that that's our job, and I'm just not sure what the truth is.

I wish it was simple. My role models have not lead me

to believe that monogamy is a natural state for long periods of time. Being happy together in a close knit situation for a very long period of time without wanting to go off and explore different things? I don't know...

NINA HARTLEY, PORN STAR:

Women are taught that they're not to have sex unless it means something. And so women talk themselves into being in love, in order to give themselves the permission to let go and enjoy a sexual encounter. Because women are not allowed to lust or to say, 'I'm horny, you're cute, I have some rubbers, let's go.'

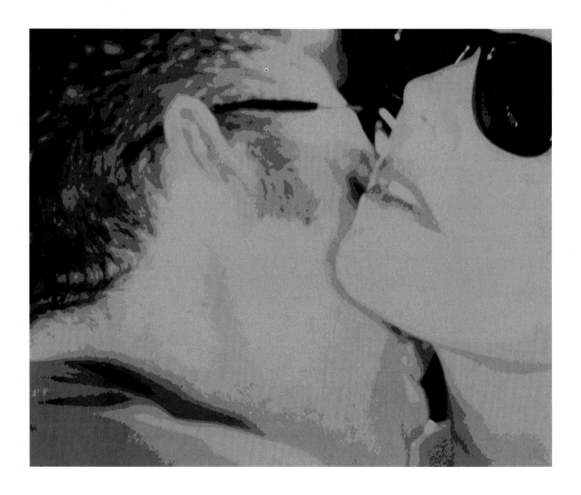

PRIVATE INVESTIGATORS

LISA STAHL:

I don't think I'd hire a private investigator to check up on someone who I thought was cheating on me because I'm so good at it myself. I've caught so many of my boyfriends cheating that I would know exactly what to do.

Here's a good trick for all women. You buy wicker floor mats for your car and you place in them little tiny sticks that stick straight up so you can tell if someone has got into the passenger side of the car. So when you ask him, 'Who was in your car today honey?' and he says 'No one honey' you'll know he's caught!

DIANE CONWAY:

I think it's a real good idea to hire a private investigator if you suspect something has happened. That's unless you have friends with time on their hands that could do it for you. You know, sit outside in an unmarked car, and see exactly what's going on. Because you can't trust everybody and if you suspect something is happening, it probably is, unless you're totally paranoid. So, go sit out there and maybe have a little secret camera in your purse. Besides, it's very exciting, isn't it?

SHERRI SPILLANE:

If I thought someone was cheating on me, I don't think I'd hire a private investigator. I'd boot them out so fast it would be a joke. But I think people who have a lot at stake may want a private investigator, to find out exactly what's going on so they have more ammunition. But I don't think I would waste his hourly rate on a cheating boyfriend. I'd just go find myself another one.

JOHN, PRIVATE INVESTIGATOR:

We're licensed by the state of California to provide private investigation services for the public. We are

...her idea was to pop a video in... and it would be him and his girlfriend.

Debra

allowed to do back investigations or follow people, serve legal papers, take pictures of people doing things they shouldn't do and court cases.

There are about a hundred different directions we can go. The most common request we get is to follow people and probably half the time it's something domestic or relationship related. Usually it's a husband or a wife that has noticed strange behaviour in their spouse. Like, a different dress, not coming home from work, going out at night, or a combination of a lot of things. They feel that something's going on and they call us.

Normally by the time a client hires us, it's because they suspect there's some fooling around going on, at least 95 per cent of the time it is.

Some people completely fall apart when we show them photographic evidence. Others go into denial and say that's not their husband on the film, even when they know it's his clothes.

I think I know why the majority of the men cheat on their wives. It's because most American women, when they hit their '30s, they cut their hair short because it's easier to care for. And it turns out that, of almost all the female clients we have, their men are fooling around with women who have longer hair then they have. And I believe that's what they're looking for.

I never find it difficult. I like to give them the information because it's usually what they want. Most of them are tired of their husbands telling them that they're not cheating on them and making them feel that they're going crazy and that all the things they think aren't really happening and that there's nothing wrong with their relationship. So, by the time they call they want us to go out and follow him and they want to know the truth. In their hearts they know it, they just need it confirmed.

Several years back it seemed that nine out of ten clients looking for this type of work were male, mostly because they controlled the purse strings and were able to write the cheques for our services. But nowadays, with more and more woman working and having access to money it's almost equal, half women, half men.

DEBRA, PRIVATE INVESTIGATOR:
I had a client call and tell us she had several micro-cassette recordings, tape after tape, of her husband talking to his girlfriend on the phone. She wanted proof with photos and on video because her husband still denied it. She couldn't admit to him that she recorded him talking because then she would lose her integrity.

So, her idea was to pop a video in to watch one night and it would be him and his girlfriend. And she thought this would be quite a fun way to get even with him.

> *It's long been said that your eyes are the mirror of the soul but it might actually be your trash.*
> JOHN

JOHN:
We do quite a bit of what's called trash nappings or garbage covers, which is going through a person's trash. I go out at night with some big hefty bags and take it away.

From trash searches, we've obtained evidence of sexual activity, narcotics use, employment when the person says they're not working, love letters, receipts. We've been able to build a picture of a person's life by going through their trash. It's said that your eyes are the mirror of the soul but it might actually be your trash.

The redial button can be very helpful in getting information. I had one lady who saw her husband on the telephone making what looked like a suspicious call and when he left the room, she went and hit redial and a woman answered at the other end and then she hung up. And she documented the time and date, waited until she got her phone bill. And what was interesting was that the phone call that she made for one minute was on

And she thought this would be a fun way to get even...

DEBRA

...of almost all the female clients, their men are fooling around with women who have longer hair...

JOHN

there, but there was no call before it which means the husband charged the call to somebody else.

CHRISTINE O'KEEFE:
Private investigation companies are helpful in a lot of areas. I feel that they should be used in some areas and not in others. I use private investigation companies to check out the basics about a new client, especially if they come to me completely unknown and I don't know anything about them. I really do want to check out if they are who they say they are, so to speak. And so, I do a background check on criminal activity, arrests, judgements, civil arrests, things like that. If they have a clean record then I'm fine. If they don't, then it's something I have to address with that potential client before I'm prepared to move forward.

If you use investigators as a surveillance tool, what you're really saying is: I don't trust you, I don't trust myself, I don't trust anyone. I think that's a matter for a psychologist to deal with before you even begin a new relationship, because if you're that suspicious of someone early on, you're going to be very suspicious of them later and that may be the demise of that relationship.

DR PAT ALLEN:
I recommend it all the time. Absolutely. I'd rather have a validated paranoid, than a paranoic without validation. I mean, honey, you got the money, hire somebody. Go get the pictures.

Because either we're going to find out you're whacko, or he's whacko, or we're going to find out there's evidence. Not that you have to do anything about the evidence. Not everybody does anything about it.

So, you've got pictures of who she is and he is and what they're doing, but the relationship is still 51 per cent valuable. So you're going to turn your head and forget it. It's just so you know. I absolutely support detectives, a good detective is worth the money they make.

JOHN:

We have one client, who is the wife, and she thinks her husband is meeting a woman today, she's overheard a conversation that they're planning to meet at a restaurant at ten this morning.

Our job is to get photographic proof of them together and then to identify the woman. Hopefully we'll see what car she comes in so we can run the plate right away and we'll try to look inside the car because most people leave things out in their car that identifies them.

This client has been recording the phone calls at home and listening to the tapes, so she's hearing his conversations and the plans he's making without him knowing, so its probably going to be a for sure.

STEPHANIE BEACHAM:

Private investigator? Hate to put anybody out of work, but I can't imagine being in that sort of mess, I just can't imagine it. Please let it never happen. Do I think that

Looks like he's happy to see her. She does have longer hair than the wife.

JOHN

they have a form of work that is worth employing? Could be. But I would hate to lead my life that fearful.

BARBARA DE ANGELIS, MARRIAGE COUNSELLOR AND THERAPIST:

If you think your partner is cheating on you, you should leave. I don't think you need a private investigator. If you already think he is behaving strangely, if you're not being loved enough, if you're not having sex, if he's mistreating you, if he refuses to go to counselling, why do you need a private investigator to tell you that it's true? You can listen to your heart and you already know whether it's true or not, that you're not happy.

SUSAN POWTER:

I think that that element of dependency and needing to find out is a false sense of control. So you find out he's screwing her, man. So what? What are you going to do? Then say, 'It's not going to make a difference.' That is all fake, and it doesn't do you any good. If you really believe that something like that is going on and you know it enough to hire someone to prove it, you already know it. Why spend the cash? Go to a spa, relax, you know, hire a lover. Do something for yourself. Don't throw the money away to find out that he's screwing a 12-year-old. Have I ever hired a detective? No. Would I ever do that? Absolutely not, no.

> *Why spend the cash?*
> *Don't throw your money away*
> *to find out that he's screwing*
> *a 12-year-old.*
>
> SUSAN POWTER

PRE-NUPTIAL AGREEMENTS

SORRELL TROPE, CELEBRITY LAWYER:
I have a personal view about pre-nuptial agreements. This is not my professional view. I don't believe, personally and emotionally, in pre-nuptials. My attitude is that if you love another individual sufficiently to marry them, you should have enough trust in them not to want to have pre-nuptial agreements signed. A pre-nuptial agreement has a very chilling effect on marriage. It's like one individual saying to the other, 'I want to marry you, but I don't really trust you to the fullest extent.'

LISA SIMMONS, JOURNALIST:
Pre-nuptials are an essential part of Hollywood marriages and that is because there's a lot of money at stake. For example, Sally Field drew up a 39-page pre-nuptial before she married her now ex-husband. It was an airtight agreement, so there were absolutely no problems when she split from him.

JOAN RIVERS:
With Jacqueline Onassis, they said the pre-nuptial was down to how many times a week she had to sleep with him.

DOUGLAS BAGBY, CELEBRITY LAWYER:
Pre-marital agreements are common among people of great wealth. They are a very good idea for certain individuals who are concerned about the consequences of the break-up of their marriage, and about the financial consequences in particular.

EMILY SCOTT-LOWE:
If you go into a relationship with a pre-nuptial agreement you're assuming that it's not going to work out. I

> *I think pre-nuptials are incredibly important in Hollywood because marriages are so short.*
>
> JACKIE COLLINS

find them very scary. You're assuming that there's not going to be a life-long commitment to the relationship, that your partner's not concerned with your own best interests. So I wonder if it doesn't get a relationship off to a bad start.

DENNIS LOWE, MARRIAGE THERAPIST:
Pre-nuptial agreements are not something that happen in middle, lower-middle or even upper-middle class homes. They're really for a unique segment of society where people have amassed great wealth and they're very concerned about being deceived and having it taken away from them.

JOAN RIVERS:
I love you, you love me, but you can't have anything of mine and I will only give you a thousand dollars if we break up. It's horrible!

STEPHANIE BEACHAM:
Isn't it hard? 'I love you. I'm going to love you for the

Pre-nuptials are an essential part of Hollywood marriages. Sally Field drew up a 39-page pre-nuptial before she married

LISA SIMMONS

rest of my life. We're going to grow old together. Do you mind signing this piece of paper, just in case?' It's a difficult one, isn't it? I would sign a pre-nuptial. Would I ask someone to sign one? Yes, I would. But maybe that's why I haven't got married, because it's a sad compromise, isn't it? When your love is tempered by that sort of reality that says, 'But just in case, honey'.

LISA STAHL:

I believe pre-nuptial agreements take away the romance from marriage and the relationship. It almost seems like you are planning the demise of your relationship before it even really gets started, but I can imagine if you were Stephen Spielberg or someone like that, you might get a little nervous about your billions of dollars. I just feel that if you are ready to marry someone and you are going to become two halves of one whole with this person, you should want to give them everything you have. If I were getting married I would want to give absolutely everything I had to them. I would be that in love with them, as you should be when you get married.

PHYLLIS DILLER, COMEDIENNE:

Banderas and Melanie Griffiths - she wanted three million if the marriage didn't last - and Banderas said, 'Look, I'm just a little Spanish kid, I don't work those kind of figures.' So right before the wedding, while she's trying on the wedding dress, they're working with the pre-nuptial and he got her down to one million. Now I think that's a horrible way to start a marriage, it has nothing to do with romance.

RHONDA:

I want a pre-nuptial that says, 'If you leave me, bastard, I get everything, you get nothing'! No really, I personally couldn't go into a marriage that way. I would be just too freaked out. That's a business deal. I guess I really do believe in true love.

Pre-nuptials are a must – don't get married without one.

BETTE MIDLER

Divorces in Hollywood can be extremely bitter.

JACKIE COLLINS

HOLLYWOOD DIVORCES AND SETTLEMENTS

DR DAVID LEVY, PSYCHOLOGIST:
For celebrities, in a sense the deck is already stacked against the likelihood of a successful marriage.

What types of people become celebrities, achieve stardom? What are they like, the people who become known as Hollywood stars, Hollywood celebrities? They are typically people who seek excitement, who crave novel stimulation, who are always looking for greener pastures. Celebrities lead very unstable lifestyles, frequently travelling, visiting different cities, shooting at various locations. It doesn't make for a stable family life when someone is away from home more frequently than they are at home, it doesn't give the family or the relationship the kind of stability that it needs to grow, to remain healthy. The lifestyle is full of temptation. It's riddled with temptation. There are exceptions but it requires particularly hard work for relationships in Hollywood to survive.

JACKIE COLINS:
I actually did insist that we got married in California because of the property laws and I figured, you know, I'd get half of everything he had. Well, silly me, I was the one who became rich and famous.

SORRELL TROPE:
A show biz divorce could be very inexpensive if both individuals want to be divorced and they have no real problems with each other. You may see a flurry in the newspapers, but the cost in terms of legal expenses is relatively minimal. On the other hand, if issues arise relating to custody and visitation of children, the cost can be quite high.

In the most expensive divorce case that this office has ever handled, the fees ran to about two and a half million dollars. That was a celebrity in the social world but not in the entertainment world. In the entertainment world I do not know of a divorce where the fees exceeded a million dollars.

I've had individuals argue over a ten dollar stove. The stove wasn't worth anything, and the judge was throwing his hands up in the air over this dispute wasting the court's time. They literally held an auction between the two individuals to determine which of them wanted the stove the most. One of them ended up paying $5,000 for this ten dollar stove. So, I mean, you get all sorts of strange arguments.

We have constant arguments over who has the right to the season tickets to the Dodger baseball games, or who has the right to the box at the Hollywood Bowl, because it is a six-person box, close up front and it takes years to get a box like that.

But probably more common is the country club membership. Although they don't have this as a published rule, a lot of country clubs will not permit a divorced husband and wife to be members of the same club. Usually the husband has the membership and so we have disputes between husbands and wives about who gets to keep the membership.

I don't know whether these are outrageous demands or not. People develop lifestyles, and they want such lifestyles to continue. I've had individuals who tell me that for the last 20, 30, or however many years, they've never actually flown on a commercial plane. And if the spouse who is providing the support can afford to, then they will charter a jet, or even buy a jet. These things all are dependent upon the financial circumstances of both parties.

I've had individuals argue over a ten dollar stove.

SORRELL TROPE

PEGGY ESTRADA, EX-WIFE ERIC ESTRADA, ACTOR:
As a celebrity wife I really lost my identity. I stopped being Peggy and I became Mrs Estrada and it was really hard to find Peggy again when he had gone because the friends and hangers-on split groups. So you can be Mrs So and So but don't lose yourself in it. It's so easy to get caught up in it, being proud of your man, being on his arm but you don't want to be jewellry.

When we were first split up I had two babies in diapers. I was completely on my own. When you're married to an actor - or anyone who is self-centered – your whole life is dedicated to them and you're part of their career and their structure. I was there to take care of him and the kids and all of a sudden he was gone.

So, I was left with these two little ones. I was pretty devastated and it wasn't like I had a whole lot of girlfriends to go running to. What I really felt was humiliated. I was like, 'What did I do wrong?' And no matter how many times you hear that it wasn't your fault, he's just messed up, you still feel bad. It took me a long time to find a support group or even just someone else who knew what I was going through.

> *What I really felt was humiliated. I was like 'What did I do wrong?'*
>
> PEGGY ESTRADA

SORRELL TROPE:
Celebrities become as emotionally involved in their divorces as anyone else. The fact that individuals are celebrities does not in anyway detract from the emotions that they feel. In fact, because of the media coverage, celebrities are far more sensitive to what is happening when they get divorced. They may be concerned about their image, how the public perceives them. This is why we have confidentiality clauses in so many agreements involving divorces among and between celebrities.

SORRELL TROPE, ON THE PHONE:

'All right, I've told you before, my client cannot possibly live on less than $50,000 a month, that's all there is to it. If it's not $50,000 a month then we are going to have to have the matter heard by the judge. I absolutely cannot take a dime less.

As for the air travel, my client absolutely must have access to the family jet. I don't care how it has to be arranged. We will arrange a certain amount of air hours a month, and we will give advance notice as to when she wants to use the plane. Well, you talk to him, and you let me know. I'll talk to you later'.

In reality this man can pay a lot more than $50,000 a month in support. He probably could afford to pay $150,000 a month in support.

OLIVIA GOLDSMITH:

Actors live a very peculiar, disjointed life. They go off to a set, they go off to a location, they're usually alone without their spouse. It's very boring work. I mean, being on a movie set even for five hours makes you want to kill yourself. They are thrown together with a bunch of very attractive strangers who know how to sell themselves because they only get a few minutes on the screen to do it, so things develop, get hot and then they go away and they don't see each other ever again.

I don't even understand what it's about now. You know, people promise to love, honour and obey and then they don't, then they do it again, then they don't, then they do it again, then don't and they do it again. I mean, what's the point?

KELLY LANGE:

This is a tragic place. People are in and out of celebrity, they're in and out of movies, they're in and out of favour and they're in and out of marriages. People meet on a movie, they are enthralled with each other, fall in love, then the movie is over, and they go their separate ways.

> *People promise to love, honour and obey and then they don't, then they do it again. I mean, what's the point?*
>
> OLIVIA GOLDSMITH

> *There's a lot of pressure put on people when they're celebrities. You're scrutinized, you have no privacy.*
>
> EMILY SCOTT-LOWE

JACKIE COLLINS:
I mean, if you have, like, $50 million, and you were going to marry a beautiful girl that you really loved, would you want to give her half of that if you got divorced in a year?

DOUGLAS BAGBY:
There are many fine lawyers in the Beverly Hills area. I would say the rates are somewhere between $250 per hour and $500 per hour. That seems to be the range.

Lisa Marie and Michael [Jackson] are very private individuals just like many other celebrities. When you represent celebrities, you have to be very sensitive to their wishes with regard to confidentiality and how much information they want disclosed. I don't encourage any of my clients to authorize me to discuss anything about their lives publicly. I believe that doing that compromises your ability to negotiate in private with the attorney representing the other side.

But to give you some idea of how quickly the press can access information, with Lisa Marie's divorce, I filed the petition at the courthouse, quite confidentially. The clerk did not even recognize the names. I handed her the check and engaged her in conversation so she didn't even see the names. She stamped the petition and put it in with the other documents to be filed. Then I left the courthouse. Before I got back to my office, only 30 minutes away, I heard a national news broadcast that Lisa Marie had filed for the dissolution of her marriage to Michael. I probably received a hundred phone calls from various press people by the end of that day.

EMILY SCOTT-LOWE:
There's a lot of pressure put on people when they're celebrities. You're scrutinized, you have no privacy. And I think it's real easy to believe that you're above everybody else and the regular rules of life just do not apply. They think they're invincible, you know, 'I command

this. I get that. I have special treatment here, there'. I think it's real easy to get self-centered. You may not have started out that way but that's not a very good attitude to bring into a marriage.

LISA SIMMONS:

The largest divorce settlement in Hollywood that I can recall probably involved Steven Spielberg and his ex-wife Amy Irving. She got $125 million for being married to him for just a few years.

Melanie Griffith is also someone who does very well for herself. I mean she went from Don [Johnson], who, you know, is quite good-looking to one of the hunkiest men on the planet, Antonio Banderas. Apparently there was some talk of a pre-nuptial between them and she balked, although maybe he got one, maybe he didn't. But, what do I think of their marriage? I doubt it will last. I'll say that on the record.

With Rosanne and Tom Arnold, you have two very volatile people as I understand. And so you get some crazy behavior during their split. You have her throwing his entire wardrobe into the pool in the backyard and then you have him saying to the judge, 'I want $150 grand for a new wardrobe.' He was denied that but he did get custody of the exercise equipment.

In exchange for your less famous spouse keeping quiet, the less famous spouse gets money that will make up for not getting a great table at Morton's anymore or not getting automatically bumped up to first class. All the things that you got and took for granted while you were married, you are given money to make up for the loss of them. And in exchange you don't talk about what happened during the marriage.

Liz Taylor and Larry Fortensky, that's another case of celebrity goodwill. He ended up getting a condo, a few million dollars and in exchange he keeps quiet. People here are very wary of having their private lives dissected in the press.

> *All the things that you got while you were married, you are given money to make up for the loss of them.*
>
> LISA SIMMONS

Charlie Sheen obviously a major party boy who does not want to grow up.

LISA SIMMONS

Kevin Costner's divorce was a very amicable one. I think he realized his wife - and this is just me supposing - had been with him from the very beginning when he was a poor struggling schmo you know, an average schmo, she stuck by him throughout.

He was not faithful. He was very much a cad according to all reports. And so I think, either because he felt his wife deserved it and he's a decent guy, or because he didn't want to have to hear about it forever after and have his wife write her autobiography, *My Life with Kevin*, he gave her half of everything including the restaurant, Twin Palms, which they owned together in Pasadena and the house in Pasadena. And it seems to have been quite a happy split.

Charlie Sheen himself has admitted to using call-girls. He's obviously a major party boy who does not want to grow up. And he has lots of money so he could afford to do it. He got married and I think the marriage lasted all of four months or something. He was given fame very young and I suppose he just doesn't want to grow up. And he's handling it in his own way. He's a case of somebody who can have anybody and if he can't have her, he'll pay for it. Then he decides to get married, finds a very attractive model and it lasts all of four months. I think maybe he wanted the experience of having a big wedding and a party in his honour. He had a very expensive wedding that was close to half a million from what I've heard. And four months later he leaves her.

And then there was David Letterman, who couldn't bear to deal with the whole divorce settlement process, so he left his wife $400 grand on the nightstand.

CHARLIE SHEEN, ACTOR
ON THE FAILURE OF HIS MARRIAGE:
You know, life goes on, right? I mean, you make a mistake and you, you own up to it and you move on.

ALANA STEWART, EX-WIFE
OF GEORGE HAMILTON AND ROD STEWART:
I think my first marriage to George didn't work because I still was very interested in, you know, the whole Hollywood life and going out and the parties and the social life and he'd done all that. We were married five years, we were together nine years and he's my best friend, he's like my family and we have a wonderful son. So I don't consider that a failure. And then I met Rod and at that point in my life I was ready to settle down. You know, he was much more into going out and being more social than I was then, which I think eventually was a problem.

PEGGY ESTRADA:
The LADIES Group - that stands for Life After Divorce is Eventually Sane (which is true though you wouldn't believe it at the beginning) - is a group of ex-wives who have been married to celebrities, famous or rich and famous people.

First of all, we support one another cause we've been through it together and if not together then successively. However, it extends way past that. We can get attention by having been married to someone with a famous last name and that puts in us a position to help other women. Our founders, Jackie and Lyn, and other women in the group go out and talk about women helping other women and getting through abusive situations. We talk about everything from help lines in your city, to one-on-

> *My first marriage to George didn't work because I was still very interested in the parties and the social life and he'd done all that.*
>
> ALANA STEWART

> *After a no-fault divorce, a woman's disposable income typically drops by 72 per cent. Men's disposable income rises by 42 per cent.*
>
> DR DAVID LEVY

one counselling, to helping other people. That's what it's really about.

It's not necessarily about our own healing any more 'cause a lot of us have gotten past that. But you never really quite do, so we're there for one another.

LYN LANDON, EX-WIFE OF MICHAEL LANDON, ACTOR:
I was married to Michael Landon for 19 years. I had a terrific marriage for, say, 17 years. Maybe Michael would have had a different answer, I don't know. But the one thing I will say is that I think you can get your priorities mixed up in marriage and once that happens, it doesn't matter who you are married to, you are going to be in deep trouble.

A divorce is painful enough. But for it to be public - and all of the stuff that is said about you is not always true either - is difficult.

But a friend once said to me, 'You can turn it off any time you want. You don't have to read it. You don't have to listen to it.' And that is one of the things I try and pass on. Even if it's a friend on the phone who wants to discuss what they read or whatever, you can always say to them, 'I prefer not to talk about this or hear about it.' Unless it's something that really involves your children or you can do something about it. Otherwise forget it. It's all just gossip.

You go through what probably every women or a man could go through. You go through devastation. You go through denial. You go through being the victim, 'Poor me'. You go through anger - I kind of liked that one 'cause I knew I was alive.

DR DAVID LEVY:
Power in marriage is primarily economic power. After a no-fault divorce, a woman's disposable income typically drops by 72 per cent. Men's disposable income rises by 42 per cent. With that in mind, people are reluctant or anxious to go through a divorce.

BARBARA DE ANGELIS:

I think because of the lifestyle of the entertainment community there's a lot of disposable relationships. Imagine what it's like: you go to Idaho to make a film for three months, and you meet somebody there and you fall in love and everything's perfect, and the press loves you. And you have no real life, you don't have a house, you don't have garbage to take out, you usually have a hundred nannies for your children, you have a fantasy life. But a lot of these relationships, where people meet on a set, tend to break up when they come back to life and they wake up in the morning and there's no one there saying, 'oh you look perfect' and, 'let me do your hair', and 'let me do your make-up'. Suddenly you're back with your personality, your goals, your dreams, the things you care about, and you may find that your compatibility with your new partner was just based on the hype and not on heart.

DAVID CARRADINE:

I find divorce to be one of the least pleasant experiences you can have, though I guess it's not as bad as going to jail. I think the process of getting a divorce is like being a little kid who has done something wrong, and he is now sitting in the principal's office waiting to find out what his punishment will be.

DOUGLAS BAGBY:

The shortest marriage I have ever heard of? There have been a number of marriages where, as soon as they were married, they wanted to dissolve it. Some of them had no intimate time together following the marriage. As soon as the ceremony was over, one or the other of them realized it was a mistake. Sometimes it's both of them and then it's just a question of: do we dissolve the marriage or do we nullify it as if we had never entered into it?

In any event, the emotions can run wild in marital dissolution matters and often do. That movie *War of the*

> *you have no real life, you don't have a house, you don't have garbage to take out, you have a fantasy life.*
>
> BARBARA DE ANGELIS

> *I've known clients who have had these immense parties to celebrate their divorce. It's more of a celebration than a wedding.*
>
> SORRELL TROPE

Roses wasn't far off the mark. Most people who saw it thought that it was very unrealistic, but those of us who are family law attorneys saw it as unfortunately very realistic because it does happen.

SORRELL TROPE:

Over the years, I've known clients who have had these immense parties to celebrate their divorce. That the trial is over. That the settlement is signed.

It's more of a celebration than a wedding. When you go to a wedding, you go out of obligation to the people that invited you, the parents, or the bride or groom, and sometimes the wedding isn't such a happy event. People who have a party to celebrate their divorce are truly happy and the party is a truly happy event.

CHRISTINE O'KEEFE:

To have been married and divorced six times is not something you should be proud of. Some people wear it like a badge of honour. 'Oh, I'm on my ninth husband'. Should I say, 'Congratulations' or 'I'm deeply sorry'? And you're never certain which one would work. You know, there are divorce cards, sold all over in card shops. 'Congratulations on your divorce.' I find this in very poor taste. I certainly don't think a divorce is anything to congratulate anyone about. Your marriage has failed. Your relationship didn't make it. Did you fail the marriage? Marriages don't fail on their own, people fail their marriage. They don't work on it nearly hard enough. They give up, and they move on. And that's very much the lie of the land in Los Angeles.

SUSAN POWTER:

I think marriages have become dispensable and I don't think that's such a bad thing. I don't believe that we have lost our morality, or that we have lost our Christian foundation, and that is why the families of America are breaking up.

I believe that women have choice now. Like I told my ex-husband, and my lover, 'I don't want your name, I got my own. I don't need your damn jewellry, I can buy my own. I don't want you to buy me flowers, 'cause I can grow my own in my garden. What I need from you is support, intimacy, and love. If you can't give me that, get the hell out 'cause, you know, you're replaceable.' I mean, you know, a penis is a penis is a penis.

DR DAVID LEVY:
It's easier to get a divorce in California than it is some other states. Particularly with no-fault divorce.

SORRELL TROPE:
I think the reason for the high divorce rate in the United States is to do with the affluence of society in general. I'm not trying to imply that only wealthy people get divorced but the level of affluence in the United States, which have grown since the end of World War II and increased dramatically over the years, has given people greater flexibility and freedom.

KELLY LANGE:
I think people are self-absorbed. They want instant gratification and, if their love life no longer involves swinging off the chandeliers, fire crackers going off and bells ringing, then they think it must be over.

DOUGLAS BAGBY:
Is divorce too easy to obtain in California? Certainly, people should work harder to stay together. They shouldn't just be able to tick a box that says, 'Irreconcilable differences' and walk away.

> *marriages have become dispensable and I don't think that's such a bad thing.*
> SUSAN POWTER

> *I don't think a divorce is anything to congratulate anyone about.*
> CHRISTINE O'KEEFE

211

We still have a lot of macho men who don't want to be told what to do. They're afraid to go to counselling.

DOYLE BARNETT

MEDIATION

DOYLE BARNETT:

I'd say the primary reason for the high level of divorce is a lack of trust. And it sounds so generic without getting into detail. But if you don't trust someone, you can't be friends with them. Friends care about each other's needs. They put the other person's needs before their own.

It seems to me that there are so many other people available, you have so many options for mates, that you are not required to make changes to make the relationship work. Rather than change yourself and go to counselling, work on yourself, to become more emotionally healthy, its just easier to find somebody else.

When I did some research, I found that in most English-speaking countries the divorce rate hovers around 50 per cent. And it seems to go up year after year.

Some of the most common problems that come up in mediation are related to family stuff, simple issues. I mean, a couple will usually come to me when they are almost ready to get a divorce and then I'll help facilitate the change.

We still have a lot of macho men who don't want to be told what to do. They don't want to be fixed, in the same way as they don't want to stop and ask directions. They're afraid to go to counselling because that means that they're wrong. That means they're going to be told what to do. And mediation hasn't got anything to do with fixing anybody. People should see it as though they have an attorney representing them. You have somebody representing your side of it, somebody who's just going to help facilitate communication.

I think there is a 95 per cent satisfaction rate in mediation in this country. But it is just in its infancy, it is just taking off. There's not as many mediators as there are attorneys, but it's being used more and more as a way of resolving conflict.

KIDS AND DIVORCE

DR DAVID LEVY, PSYCHOLOGIST:
When one parent plays a child against the other spouse, it's almost always bad for the child. So, despite the fact that a parent may have negative feelings about his or her ex, it's important to keep those in check for the benefit of the child.

SORRELL TROPE:
I think divorce is a very traumatic event for the children of the marriage, and I don't know that there is a best way to handle it.

Assuming you've got children who are emotionally equipped to handle it, it's best for both the parents to sit down together with the children and inform them that the divorce has nothing to do with them and that both parents still love them. Unfortunately there are a lot of people in this world who are either unwilling to have that sort of dialogue with children, or who have a far more sinister agenda and engage in parental alienation, that is, where one spouse tries to poison or alienate the children against the other spouse. That is far more common than the individuals who sit down calmly with the children and explain that the children are not the cause of the divorce.

ALEXANDRA PAUL, ACTRESS, *BAYWATCH*:
I don't believe it was my parents divorce that affected me, but their unhappy marriage, the lack of love between them. Because my parents' divorce was incredibly civil and they loved us so much. So I wanted them to get divorced, because I hated the tension in the house.

I always knew my parents loved me even if they didn't love each other. So I'd never recommend that people stay together for the kids. My parents are both great parents, just weren't great for each other.

> *I actually wanted them to get divorced, because I hated the tension in the house.*
>
> ALEXANDRA PAUL

> *Everybody would want a Shakespeare baby. It would be great! To get that creative juice, it would be wonderful.*
>
> DIANE CONWAY

LIFE WITHOUT MEN

DIANE CONWAY:

When people go along to the sperm bank they choose somebody that they want the characteristics of, like Einstein's intelligence. If only Einstein had jacked off in a bottle, wouldn't that be great? Or Shakespeare, can you imagine? Everybody would want a Shakespeare baby. It would be great! To get that creative juice, it would be wonderful.

We should make a mandatory law that all of our present geniuses and artists and actors have to do it in a bottle so that we have a really nice bank. And perhaps mix some traits together, you know, do a little blending, a kind of cocktail.

The best way to do it - and I know several people that have gotten impregnated this way - is to use a turkey baster. You take a turkey baster and you squeeze it and it goes up and it's pretty much the right size. I know two people who used that, I know the babies, they came out just fine, lovely babies.

JACKIE COLLINS:

Sperm donors – they love donating 'cause they get to go in that little room with *Playboy* magazine and it makes them all happy.

DR GRAHAM, WHO RUNS A SPERM BANK:

I'm constantly on the alert. I go to scientific meetings. I go to public meetings. I read the literature. I ask for referrals from hundreds of friends and other people who are interested. We get the identification of some outstanding men and I approach them. I ask them if they'll be a sperm donor. No man is hurt by being asked. Most of them turn me down, of course, but some of them agree, so we have a certain number, a couple of dozen, from these outstanding donors.

BARBARA DE ANGELIS:

Are sperm banks a good idea? For the donor or for the recipient? I think that if a woman's married and her husband does not have viable sperm and they wanted to have a child, there's nothing wrong with going to a sperm bank.

I happen to have a very strong, spiritual belief that if a child ends up here, then it was destined to be here, however it comes, whether through a sperm bank or through in vitro fertilization, or through a surrogate. God put them here and they've made it and and they're a miracle.

So, I don't think there's anything wrong with sperm banks. Although I do think shopping from one sperm bank to another, trying to find pictures of the perfect man starts to sound a little bit like Nazi Germany and that's a little scary.

DR GRAHAM:

Some of our donors are more popular than others. Some of them are young gods, they have it all to a superlative degree: they're huge and magnificent and healthy and bright and have a fine background. They just are lucky people and they share this good fortune with lots of little children.

SUSAN POWTER:

The perfect man via test tube super sperm bank? I've never even thought about that. It's never been a prerequisite for me. Have my Little Einstein in a tube? I don't know. If that's important to you, fine. What's more important to me is not having the perfect child, it's getting as close as you can to being a loving, committed parent. So what if the kid has a genius IQ?

A super sperm bank? No. You don't need perfecion. You need fabric and texture and life and problems. You don't want perfect, there's no such thing. Super sperm banks, they're a lie.

> *In my younger days maybe I would want one from Antonio Banderas.*
>
> SHERRI SPILLANE

215

ACKNOWLEDGEMENTS

The publishers would like to thank Mike Morris and Kylie Hendry at ITEL.

September Films would like to thank producer Jannine Waddell, director David Cummings, executive producer David Green and everyone involved in the making of the *Hollywood Lovers* series, especially Michael Conn, Burrell Durrant Hifle, Fiona Alderson, Donna Adcock, Chris Kenyon, Stephen Cookman, Nick Adams, Adam Edsall, Peter Sarandon, Lysette Cohen, Elaine Day, Elliot Cowand, Bryan Hall, Ewen Thomson, Paul Jarvis, Margaret Ward, Polly Leach and Jo Molloy. Special thanks to photographer Eddie Sanderson.

PICTURE CREDITS

Eddie Sanderson
Pages 10, 22, 58, 66, 95, 187, 210

Rex Features International
Front cover, page 46

Capital Pictures
Pages 126, 130, 170, 174

London Features
Front cover, page 2

The Kobal Collection
Page 134

Katz Pictures
Page 146